Ally the Alligator

1st Generation

The Beanie Babies Collection
[Beanie Name]™ [Style Number]
© 1993 Ty Inc. Oakbrook, IL, USA
All Rights Reserved. Caution:
Remove this tag before giving
toy to a child. For ages 5 and up.
Handmade in Korea.
Surface
Wash

2nd Generation

The Beanie Babies Collection
© 1993 Ty Inc. Oakbrook, IL, USA
All Rights Reserved.
Remove this tag before giving
toy to a child. For ages 3 and up
Handmade in China
Surface
Wash

[Beanie Name]™ [Style Number]
to_____
from_____
with
love

3rd Generation

The Beanie Babies ™ Collection
© Ty Inc.
Oakbrook IL. U.S.A.
© Ty UK Ltd.
Waterlooville, Hants
PO8 8NH
© Ty Deutschland
90008 Nürnberg
Handmade in China

[Beanie Name]™ [Style Number]
to_____
from_____
with
love

4th Generation

The Beanie Babies™ Collection
© Ty Inc.
Oakbrook IL. U.S.A.
© Ty UK Ltd.
Fareham, Hants
PO15 5TX
© Ty Deutschland
90008 Nürnberg
Handmade in China

[Beanie Name]™ [Style Number]
DATE OF BIRTH: [Month-Day-Year]
[Beanie Poem]
Visit our web page!!!
http://www.ty.com

Ally the Alligator was retired in October 1997.

Item #: 4032
Issued: 1994
Retired: 10/97
Birthday: 3/14/94

When Ally gets out of classes
He wears a hat and dark glasses
He plays bass in a street band
He's the coolest gator in the land!

Baldy the Eagle

Collectors interested in a patriotic theme should consider adding Baldy to Lefty, Righty and Libearty for a display.

Item #: 4074
Issued: 1997
Birthday: 2/17/96

Hair on his head is quite scant
We suggest Baldy get a transplant
Watching over the land of the free
Hair in his eyes would make it hard to see!

Beanie Collector Guide

Published by
Trend Masters Publication • Grand Rapids, Michigan

Publisher: Jeffrey R. Beckett

Editor: Jay Johnson

Art Director: Lisa O'Neill

Contributing Editors: Jeff Czerniakowski, Kim Goddard, Sharon E. Johnson, Vicky Krupka

Photography: Rebecca Reed, Daniel Harris, Jeff Sciortino

Cover photo by Rebecca Reed

Published by

Trend Masters Publication
2432 Oakwood Drive SE
Grand Rapids, MI 49506

Manufactured in the United States of America

ISBN: 0-9662573-1-6

First Edition: April 1998

10 9 8 7 6 5 4 3 2 1

Table of Contents

Batty the Bat

Batty replaced the popular retiree Radar in the collection.

Item #: 4035

Issued: 1997

Birthday: 10/29/96

Bats may make some people jitter
Please don't be scared of this critter
If you're lonely or have nothing to do
This Beanie Baby would love to hug you!

Bernie the St. Bernard

4th Generation

5th Generation

As one of the lower priced Beanies, Bernie is a wonder-ful starting place for a Beanie dogs collection.

Item #: 4109
Issued: 1997
Birthday: 10/3/96

This little dog can't wait to grow
To rescue people lost in snow
Don't let him out - keep him on your shelf
He doesn't know how to rescue himself!

Bessie the Brown Cow

3rd Generation

4th Generation

Bessie the Brown Cow was retired in October 1997.

Item #: 4009
Issued: 1995
Retired: 10/97
Birthday: 6/27/95

Bessie the cow likes to dance and sing
Because music is her favorite thing
Every night when you are counting sheep
She'll sing you a song to help you sleep!

Blackie the Black Bear

1st Generation

2nd Generation

3rd Generation

4th Generation

5th Generation

Current versions of Blackie are among the most accessible of the Beanie bears.

Item #: 4011
Issued: 1994
Birthday: 7/15/94

Living in a national park
He only played after dark
Then he met his friend Cubbie
Now they play when it's sunny!

Blizzard the White Tiger

Blizzard debuted on Mother's Day 1997 and is constructed just like Stripes, albeit in white instead of yellow.

Item #: 4163
Issued: 1997
Birthday: 12/12/96

In the mountains where it's snowy and cold
Lives a beautiful tiger, I've been told
Black and white, she's hard to compare
Of all the tigers, she is the most rare.

Bones the Dog

1st Generation

The Beanie Babies Collection
[Beanie Name]™ [Style Number]
© 1993 Ty Inc. Oakbrook, IL USA
All Rights Reserved. Caution:
Remove this tag before giving
toy to a child. For ages 5 and up.
Handmade in Korea.
Surface
Wash.

2nd Generation

The Beanie Babies Collection
© 1993 Ty Inc. Oakbrook, IL USA
All Rights Reserved. Caution:
Remove this tag before giving
toy to a child. For ages 3 and up.
Handmade in China.
Surface
Wash.

[Beanie Name]™ [Style Number]
to _____
from_____
with
love

3rd Generation

The Beanie Babies ™ Collection
© Ty Inc.
Oakbrook IL. U.S.A.
© Ty UK Ltd.
Waterlooville, Hants
P08 8HH
© Ty Deutschland
90008 Nürnberg
Handmade in China

[Beanie Name]™ [Style Number]
to _____
from ____
with
love

4th Generation

The Beanie Babies™ Collection
© Ty Inc.
Oakbrook IL. U.S.A.
© Ty UK Ltd.
Fareham, Hants
PO15 5TX
© Ty Deutschland
90008 Nürnberg
Handmade in China

[Beanie Name]™ [Style Number]
DATE OF BIRTH: [Month-Day-Year]

[Beanie Poem]

Visit our web page!!!
http://www.ty.com

5th Generation

The Beanie Babies Collection
© Ty Inc.
Oakbrook, IL. U.S.A.
© Ty Europe Ltd
Fareham, Hants
PO15 5TX
Ty Canada
Aurora, Ontario
Handmade in China

[Beanie Name]™
DATE OF BIRTH: [Month-Day-Year]

[Beanie Poem]

www.ty.com

Please remove all swing tags
before giving this item to a child

Action Toy For Reference
For ages 3 and up
Surface
Wash

> Bones is one of the few
> Beanies to have featured all
> five generations of tags.

Item #: 4001
Issued: 1995
Birthday: 1/18/94

Bones is a dog that loves to chew
Chairs and a table and a smelly old shoe
"You're so destructive" all would shout
But that all stopped when his teeth fell out!

Bongo the Monkey

1st Generation

The Beanie Babies Collection
[Beanie Name]™ [Style Number]
©1993 Ty Inc. Oakbrook, IL, USA
All Rights Reserved. Caution:
Remove this tag before giving
toy to a child. For ages 5 and up.
Handmade in Korea.
Surface
Wash.

2nd Generation

The Beanie Babies Collection
© 1993 Ty Inc. Oakbrook, IL, USA
All Rights Reserved. Caution:
Remove this tag before giving
toy to a child. For ages 3 and up.
Handmade in China
Surface
Wash.

[Beanie Name]™ [Style Number]
to _____
from _____
with
love

3rd Generation

The Beanie Babies ™ Collection
© Ty Inc.
Oakbrook IL. U.S.A.
© Ty UK Ltd.
Waterlooville, Hants
PO8 8HH
© Ty Deutschland
90008 Nürnberg
Handmade in China

[Beanie Name]™ [Style Number]
to _____
from _____
with
love

4th Generation

The Beanie Babies™ Collection
© Ty Inc.
Oakbrook IL. U.S.A.
© Ty UK Ltd.
Fareham, Hants
PO15 5TX
© Ty Deutschland
90008 Nürnberg
Handmade in China

[Beanie Name]™ [Style Number]
DATE OF BIRTH: [Month-Day-Year]
[Beanie Poem]
Visit our web page!!!
http://www.ty.com

5th Generation

The Beanie Babies Collection
© Ty Inc.
Oakbrook, IL. U.S.A.
© Ty Europe Ltd.
Fareham, Hants
PO15 5TX
© Ty Canada
Nursery, Ontario
Handmade in China

Please remove all swing tags
before giving this item to a child

[Beanie Name]™
DATE OF BIRTH: [Month-Day-Year]
[Beanie Poem]
www.ty.com

Bongo was introduced with his tail the same color as his body with old tags. Then his tail was the same color as his face with old tags. He stayed this way with a switch to new tags until recently, when he was reinstated with body and tail once again matching.

Item #: 4067
Issued: 1995
Birthday: 8/17/95

Bongo the Monkey lives in a tree
The happiest monkey you'll ever see
In his spare time he plays the guitar
One of these days he will be a big star!

11

Britannia the Bear
(European Exclusive)

5th Generation

Issued in 1998, Britannia was a huge hit. Ty has gone to great lengths to try and keep it from entering the U.S., driving up market prices.

Issued: 1/98
Birthday: 12/15/97

Britannia the bear will sail the sea
So she can be with you and me
She's always sure to catch the tide
And wear the Union Flag with pride

Bronty the Brontosaurus

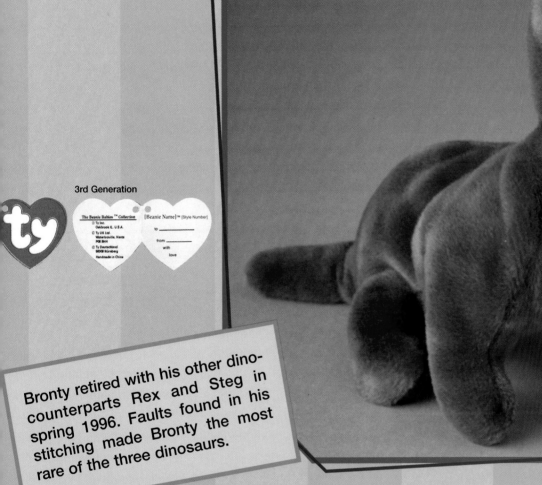

3rd Generation

ty

The Beanie Babies ™ Collection
© Ty Inc.
Oakbrook IL. U.S.A.
© Ty UK Ltd.
Waterlooville, Hants
P08 8HH
© Ty Deutschland
90008 Nürnberg
Handmade in China

[Beanie Name]™ [Style Number]
to _____
from _____
with
love

Bronty retired with his other dino-counterparts Rex and Steg in spring 1996. Faults found in his stitching made Bronty the most rare of the three dinosaurs.

No Poem

Item #: 4085

Issued: 1995

Retired: 1996

Birthday: Unknown

13

Bruno the Terrier

5th Generation

Bruno led the New Year's Day parade of 1998 introductions.

Issued: 1/98
Birthday: 9/9/97

Bruno the dog thinks he's a brute
But all the other Beanies think he's cute
He growls at his tail and runs in a ring
And everyone says, "Oh, how darling!"

Bubbles the Fish

3rd Generation

The Beanie Babies ™ Collection
① Ty Inc.
Oakbrook IL. U.S.A.
⑥ Ty UK Ltd.
Waterlooville, Hants
PO8 8HH
⑧ Ty Deutschland
90008 Nürnberg
Handmade in China

[Beanie Name]™ [Style Number]

to _____
from _____
with
love

4th Generation

The Beanie Babies™ Collection
① Ty Inc.
Oakbrook IL. U.S.A.
⑥ Ty UK Ltd.
Fareham, Hants
PO15 5TX
⑧ Ty Deutschland
90008 Nürnberg
Handmade in China

[Beanie Name]™ [Style Number]
DATE OF BIRTH : [Month-Day-Year]

[Beanie Poem]

Visit our web page!!!
http://www.ty.com

Bubbles was retired in May 1997.

Item #: 4078
Issued: 1995
Retired: 5/97
Birthday: 7/2/95

All day long Bubbles likes to swim
She never gets tired of flapping her fins
Bubbles lived in a sea of blue
Now she is ready to come home with you!

Bucky the Beaver

3rd Generation

The Beanie Babies ™ Collection
© Ty Inc.
Oakbrook IL. U.S.A.
© Ty UK Ltd.
Waterlooville, Hants
PO8 8HH
© Ty Deutschland
90008 Nürnberg
Handmade in China

[Beanie Name]™ [Style Number]
to _____
from _____
with
love

4th Generation

The Beanie Babies™ Collection
© Ty Inc.
Oakbrook IL. U.S.A.
© Ty UK Ltd.
Fareham, Hants
PO15 5TX
© Ty Deutschland
90008 Nürnberg
Handmade in China

[Beanie Name]™ [Style Number]
DATE OF BIRTH: [Month-Day-Year]

[Beanie Poem]

Visit our web page!!!
http://www.ty.com

Bucky retired in January 1998.

Item #: 4016
Issued: 1995
Retired: 1/98
Birthday: 6/8/95

Bucky's teeth are as shiny as can be
Often used for cutting trees
He hides in his dam night and day
Maybe for you he will come out and play!

16

Bumble the Bee

Bumble the Bee retired in spring 1996.

Item #: 4045
Issued: 1995
Retired: 1996
Birthday: 10/16/95

Bumble the bee will not sting you
It is only love that this bee will bring you
So don't be afraid to give this bee a hug
Because Bumble the bee is a love-bug.

17

Caw the Crow

3rd Generation

The Beanie Babies ™ Collection   [Beanie Name]™ [Style Number]
© Ty Inc.
Oakbrook IL. U.S.A.   to _____
© Ty UK Ltd.
Waterlooville, Hants   from _____
PO8 9HH
© Ty Deutschland   with
90008 Nürnberg
Handmade in China   love

Caw the Crow retired in spring 1996.

Poem: None

Item #: 4071

Issued: 1995

Retired: 1996

Birthday: Unknown

18

Chilly the Polar Bear

1st Generation

The Beanie Babies Collection
[Beanie Name]™ [Style Number]
© 1993 Ty Inc. Oakbrook, IL USA
All Rights Reserved. Caution:
Remove this tag before giving
toy to a child. For ages 5 and up.
Handmade in Korea.
Surface
Wash.

2nd Generation

The Beanie Babies Collection
© 1993 Ty Inc. Oakbrook, IL. USA
All Rights Reserved. Caution:
Remove this tag before giving
toy to a child. For ages 3 and up.
Handmade in China.
Surface
Wash.

[Beanie Name]™ [Style Number]
to _____
from _____
with love

3rd Generation

The Beanie Babies ™ Collection
① Ty Inc.
Oakbrook IL. U.S.A.
② Ty UK Ltd.
Waterlooville, Hants
PO8 8HH
③ Ty Deutschland
90008 Nürnberg
Handmade in China

[Beanie Name]™ [Style Number]
to _____
from _____
with
love

Chilly the Polar Bear
retired in spring 1996.

Poem: None

Item #: 4012

Issued: 1995

Retired: 1996

Birthday: Unknown

19

Chip

the Calico Cat

4th Generation

5th Generation

Chip was introduced in May 1997.

Item #: 4121
Issued: 1997
Birthday: Unknown

Black and gold, brown and white
The shades of her coat are quite a sight
At mixing her colors she was a master
On anyone else it would be a disaster!

Chocolate the Moose

1st Generation

2nd Generation

3rd Generation

4th Generation

5th Generation

One of the original nine, Chocolate has ridden the wave of all generations of tags without undergoing cosmetic reconstruction.

Item #: 4015
Issued: 1994
Birthday: 4/27/93

Licorice, gum and peppermint candy
This moose always has these handy
But there is one more thing he likes to eat
Can you guess his favorite sweet?

Chops the Lamb

Chops the Lamb was retired in January 1997, possibly to avoid a lawsuit with Shari Lewis over her Lambchop TV character.

Item #: 4019
Issued: 1996
Retired: 1997

Chops is a little lamb
This lamb you'll surely know
Because every path that you may take
This lamb is sure to go!

Claude the Crab

4th Generation

5th Generation

Claude was introduced in May 1997. As Digger retired, Claude became his tie-dyed successor. He appears to be a darker stain than earlier tie-dyes.

Item #: 4083

Issued: 1997

Birthday: 9/3/96

Claude the crab paints by the sea
A famous artist he hopes to be
But the tide came in and his paints fell
Now his art is on his shell!

Congo the Gorilla

For some reason, Congo has never been particularly popular or expensive. He may be a target for retirement in the near future.

Item #: 4160

Issued: 1996

Birthday: 11/9/96

Black as night and fierce is he
On the ground or in a tree
Strong and mighty as the Congo
He's related to our Bongo!

Coral the Fish

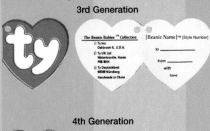
Coral the Fish retired in January 1997.

Item #: 4079
Issued: 1995
Retired: 1/97
Birthday: 3/2/95

Coral is beautiful, as you know
Made of colors in the rainbow
Whether it's pink, yellow or blue
These colors were chosen just for you!

25

Crunch the Shark

Crunch was introduced in January 1997. He has the honor of being the only Beanie Baby with fierce felt teeth.

Item #: 4130
Issued: 1997
Birthday: 1/13/96

What's for breakfast? What's for lunch?
Yum? Delicious! Munch, munch, munch!
He's eating everything by the bunch
That's the reason we named him Crunch!

Cubbie the Brown Bear

1st Generation

The Beanie Babies Collection
[Beanie Name]™ [Style Number]
© 1993 Ty Inc. Oakbrook, IL USA
All Rights Reserved. Caution:
Remove this tag before giving
toy to a child. For ages 5 and up.
Handmade in Korea.
Surface
Wash.

2nd Generation

The Beanie Babies Collection
[Beanie Name]™ [Style Number]
© 1993 Ty Inc. Oakbrook, IL. USA
All Rights Reserved. Caution:
Remove this tag before giving
toy to a child. For ages 3 and up.
Handmade in China
Surface
Wash

to _____
from _____
with
love

3rd Generation

The Beanie Babies ™ Collection
① Ty Inc.
Oakbrook IL. U.S.A.
② Ty UK Ltd.
Waterlooville, Hants
P08 8HH
③ Ty Deutschland
90008 Nürnberg
Handmade in China

[Beanie Name]™ [Style Number]
to _____
from _____
with
love

4th Generation

The Beanie Babies™ Collection
① Ty Inc.
Oakbrook IL. U.S.A.
② Ty UK Ltd.
Fareham, Hants
P015 5TX
③ Ty Deutschland
90008 Nürnberg
Handmade in China

[Beanie Name]™ [Style Number]
DATE OF BIRTH: [Month-Day-Year]
[Beanie Poem]

Visit our web page!!!
http://www.ty.com

Cubbie became the fifth of the original nine to retire when he departed the stage in January 1998.

Item #: 4010
Issued: 1994
Retired: 1/98
Birthday: 11/14/93

Cubbie used to eat crackers and honey
And what happened to him was funny
He was stung by fourteen bees
Now Cubbie eats broccoli and cheese.

27

Curly the Napped Bear

4th Generation

5th Generation

Curly was introduced in spring 1996 and, with Scottie, is one of the first napped Beanies ever made. Curly also has the distinction of being the only napped bear in the collection.

Item #: 4052
Issued: 1996
Birthday: 4/12/96

A bear so cute with hair that's curly
You will love and want him surely
To this bear always be true
He will be a friend to you!

28

Daisy the Black & White Cow

1st Generation

The Beanie Babies Collection
[Beanie Name]™ [Style Number]
© 1993 Ty Inc. Oakbrook, IL USA
All Rights Reserved. Caution:
Remove this tag before giving
toy to a child. For ages 5 and up.
Handmade in Korea.
Surface
Wash.

2nd Generation

The Beanie Babies Collection
© 1993 Ty Inc. Oakbrook, IL USA
Remove this tag before giving
toy to a child. For ages 3 and up.
Handmade in China.
Surface.
Wash.

[Beanie Name]™ [Style Number]
to _____
from _____
with
love

3rd Generation

The Beanie Babies ™ Collection
① Ty Inc.
Oakbrook IL. U.S.A.
② Ty UK Ltd.
Waterlooville, Hants
PO8 8HH
③ Ty Deutschland
90008 Nürnberg
Handmade in China

[Beanie Name]™ [Style Number]
to _____
from _____
with
love

4th Generation

The Beanie Babies™ Collection
① Ty Inc.
Oakbrook IL. U.S.A.
② Ty UK Ltd.
Fareham, Hants
PO15 5TX
③ Ty Deutschland
90008 Nürnberg
Handmade in China

[Beanie Name]™ [Style Number]
DATE OF BIRTH: [Month-Day-Year]

[Beanie Poem]

Visit our web page!!!
http://www.ty.com

5th Generation

The Beanie Babies Collection
① Ty Inc.
Oakbrook, IL. U.S.A
② Ty Europe Ltd
Fareham, Hants
PO15 5TX
③ Ty Canada
Aurora, Ontario
Handmade in China

Please remove all swing tags
before giving this item to a child

Swing Tag for Reference
For ages 3 and up
Surface
Wash

[Beanie Name]™
DATE OF BIRTH: [Month-Day-Year]

[Beanie Poem]

www.ty.com

Daisy has worn all five generations of tags at relatively inexpensive prices. Owning all five versions would be a low-priced way to own examples of all the tags.

Item #: 4006
Issued: 1994
Birthday: 5/10/94

Daisy drinks milk each night
So her coat is shiny and bright
Milk is good for your hair and skin
What a way for your day to begin!

Derby the Horse

There are three versions of this horse: with a fine-yarn mane and tail, with a coarse-yarn mane and tail, and the current version with a star on its forehead.

Item #: 4008
Issued: 1995
Birthday: 9/16/95

All the other horses used to tattle
Because Derby never wore his saddle
He left the stables, and the horses too
Just so Derby can be with you!

Digger

the Crab (Old - Orange, New - Red)

1st Generation

2nd Generation

3rd Generation

4th Generation

Digger retired in May 1997 so Claude the Crab could take its place as the tie-dyed crab.

Item #: 4027
Issued: 1995
Retired: 5/97
Birthday: 8/23/95

Digging in the sand and walking sideways
That's how Digger spends her days
Hard on the outside but sweet deep inside
Basking in the sun, riding the tide!

Doby the Doberman

4th Generation

The Beanie Babies™ Collection
© Ty Inc.
  Oakbrook IL. U.S.A.
© Ty UK Ltd.
  Farnham, Hants
  P015 STX
© Ty Deutschland
  90008 Nürnberg
Handmade in China

[Beanie Name]™ [Style Number]
DATE OF BIRTH: [Month-Day-Year]

[Beanie Poem]

Visit our web page!!
http://www.ty.com

5th Generation

The Beanie Babies Collection®
© Ty Inc.
  Oakbrook, IL U.S.A.
  Ty Europe Ltd.
  Farnham, Hants
  P015 STX
  Ty Canada
  Aurora, Ontario
  Handmade in China

[Beanie Name]™
DATE OF BIRTH: [Month-Day-Year]

[Beanie Poem]

www.Ty.com

Please remove all swing tags
before giving this item to a child
Return Tag for reference
For ages 3 and up
Surface
Wash

Doby is one of the favorite Beanies for many male collectors.

Item #: 4110
Issued: 1997
Birthday: 10/9/96

This dog is little but he has might
Keep him close when you sleep at night
He lays around with nothing to do
Until he sees it's time to protect you!

Dotty the Dalmatian

4th Generation

4th Generation

5th Generation

Dotty was introduced on Mother's Day 1997 and replaced Sparky the Dalmatian. Her arrival was not Ty's best-kept secret, as final shipments of Sparky the Dalmatian arrived in stores with Dotty tush tags.

Item #: 4100
Issued: 1997
Birthday: 10/17/96

The Beanies all thought it was a big joke
While writing her tag, their ink pen broke
She got in the way, and got all spotty
So now the Beanies call her Dotty!

Ears the Rabbit

3rd Generation

4th Generation

5th Generation

Ears makes an excellent Easter present for new or would-be collectors.

Item #: 4018
Issued: 1996
Birthday: 4/18/95

He's been eating carrots so long
Didn't understand what was wrong
Couldn't see the board during classes
Until the doctor gave him glasses!

Echo the Dolphin

4th Generation

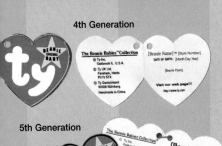

5th Generation

Echo the Dolphin was introduced in May 1997 as Flash's replacement.

Item #: 4180
Issued: 1997
Birthday: 12/21/96

Echo the dolphin lives in the sea
Playing with her friends, like you and me
Through the waves she echoes the sound
"I'm so glad to have you around!"

Erin the Bear

5th Generation

Erin and Princess are the only two Beanies introduced as solo acts. Erin debuted to celebrate the St. Patrick's Day holiday, sparking a mad dash to stores.

Issued: 3/98
Birthday: 3/17/97

Named after the beautiful Emerald Isle
This Beanie Baby will make you smile,
A bit of luck, a pot of gold,
Light up the faces, both yound and old!

Flash the Dolphin

1st Generation

The Beanie Babies Collection
[Beanie Name]™ [Style Number]
© 1993 Ty Inc. Oakbrook, IL, USA
All Rights Reserved. Caution:
Remove this tag before giving
toy to a child. For ages 3 and up.
Handmade in Korea
Surface
Wash

2nd Generation

The Beanie Babies Collection
[Beanie Name]™ [Style Number]
© 1993 Ty Inc. Oakbrook, IL, USA
All Rights Reserved. Caution:
Remove this tag before giving
toy to a child. For ages 3 and up.
Handmade in China
Surface
Wash
to _____
from _____
with
love

3rd Generation

The Beanie Babies ™ Collection
© Ty Inc.
Oakbrook IL. U.S.A.
© Ty UK Ltd.
Waterlooville, Hants
PO8 8HH
© Ty Deutschland
90008 Nürnberg
Handmade in China
[Beanie Name]™ [Style Number]
to _____
from _____
with
love

4th Generation

The Beanie Babies™ Collection
© Ty Inc.
Oakbrook IL. U.S.A.
© Ty UK Ltd.
Fareham, Hants
PO15 5TX
© Ty Deutschland
90008 Nürnberg
Handmade in China
[Beanie Name]™ [Style Number]
DATE OF BIRTH : [Month-Day-Year]
[Beanie Poem]
Visit our web page!!!
http://www.ty.com

Retired in May 1997, Flash made way for Echo the Dolphin. Echo has a definite curve, as if he's jumping out of the water, while Flash lies flat.

Item #: 4021
Issued: 1994
Retired: 5/97
Birthday: 5/13/93

You know dolphins are a smart breed
Our friend flash knows how to read
Splash the whale is the one who taught her
Although reading is difficult under the water.

37

Fleece the Lamb

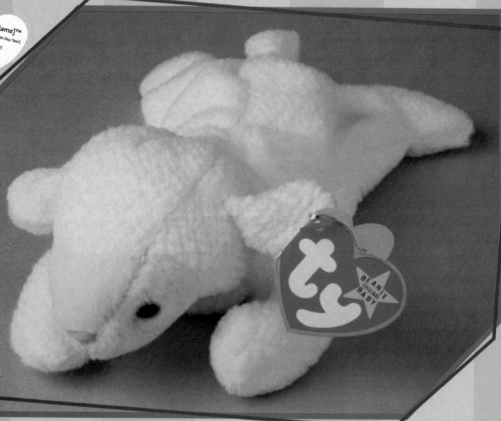

As Chops left the limelight and retired in January 1997, Fleece took her place. Chops had a black face, whereas Fleece's face is a light taupe color similar to Snip the Cat's body.

Item #: 4125
Issued: 1997
Birthday: 3/21/96

Fleece would like to sing a lullaby
Please be patient, she's really shy
When you sleep, keep her by your ear
Her song will leave you nothing to fear.

38

Flip the Cat

3rd Generation

4th Generation

Flip the White Cat was retired in October 1997.

Item #: 4012
Issued: 1996
Retired: 10/97
Birthday: 2/28/95

Flip the cat is an acrobat
She loves playing on her mat
This cat flips with such grace and flair
She can somersault in midair.

Floppity the Lavender Bunny

4th Generation

5th Generation

Floppity, Hippity and Hoppity always seem to find their way into Easter baskets in the spring.

Item #: 4118
Issued: 1997
Birthday: 5/28/96

Floppity hops from here to there
Searching for eggs without a care
Lavender coat from head to toe
All dressed up and nowhere to go!

40

Flutter the Butterfly

3rd Generation

Flutter the Butterfly was retired in spring 1996.

Poem: None

Item #: 4043

Issued: 1995

Retired: 1996

Birthday: Unknown

Freckles the Leopard

4th Generation

5th Generation

Freckles has always been easily available, but his spotted design still makes him popular.

Item #: 4066
Issued: 1996
Birthday: 6/3/96

From the trees he hunts his prey
In the night and in the day
He's the king of camouflage
Look real close, he's no mirage!

Garcia
the Bear

Garcia was retired in May 1997. According to rumor, production of Garcia was stopped to avoid litigation with the Jerry Garcia estate. Since the tie-dyed bear was so popular, Peace took his place.

Item #: 4051
Issued: 1995
Retired: 5/97
Birthday: 8/1/95

The Beanies used to follow him around
Because Garcia traveled from town to town
He's pretty popular as you can see
Some even say he's legendary.

Gobbles the Turkey

5th Generation

The Beanie Babies™ Collection

Gobbles debuted in time for Thanksgiving 1997.

Item #: 4034
Issued: 1997
Birthday: 11/27/96

Gobbles the turkey loves to eat
Once a year she has a feast
I have a secret I'd like to divulge
If she eats too much her tummy will bulge!

Goldie the Goldfish

1st Generation

The Beanie Babies Collection
[Beanie Name]™ [Style Number]
© 1993 Ty Inc. Oakbrook, IL USA
All Rights Reserved. Caution:
Remove this tag before giving
toy to a child. For ages 5 and up
Handmade in Korea.
Surface
Wash

2nd Generation

The Beanie Babies Collection
© 1993 Ty Inc. Oakbrook IL. U.S.A.
All Rights Reserved. Caution:
Remove this tag before giving
toy to a child. For ages 3 and up.
Handmade in China
Surface
Wash.

[Beanie Name]™ [Style Number]
to _____
from _____
with
love

3rd Generation

The Beanie Babies ™ Collection
© Ty Inc.
Oakbrook IL. U.S.A.
© Ty UK Ltd.
Waterlooville, Hants
PO8 8HH
© Ty Deutschland
90008 Nürnberg
Handmade in China

[Beanie Name]™ [Style Number]
to _____
from _____
with
love

4th Generation

The Beanie Babies™ Collection
© Ty Inc.
Oakbrook, IL. U.S.A.
© Ty UK Ltd.
Fareham, Hants
PO15 5TX
© Ty Deutschland
90008 Nürnberg
Handmade in China

[Beanie Name]™ [Style Number]
DATE OF BIRTH [Month-Day-Year]

[Beanie Poem]

Visit our web page!!!
http://www.ty.com

Goldie swam off into retirement in January 1998.

Item #: 4023
Issued: 1994
Retired: 1/98
Birthday: 11/14/94

She's got rhythm, she's got soul
What more to like in a fish bowl?
Through sound waves Goldie swam
Because this goldfish likes to jam!

Gracie the Swan

4th Generation

5th Generation

This graceful bird was added to the line-up in 1997.

Item #: 4126
Issued: 1997
Birthday: 6/17/96

As a duckling, she was confused
Birds on the lake were quite amused
Poking fun until she would cry,
Now the most beautiful swan at Ty!

Grunt the Razorback

3rd Generation

The Beanie Babies™ Collection
- Ty Inc. Oakbrook IL, U.S.A.
- Ty UK Ltd. Waterlooville, Hants PO8 8HH
- Ty Deutschland 90008 Nürnberg

Handmade in China

[Beanie Name]™ [Style Number]

to _____

from _____

with

love

4th Generation

The Beanie Babies™ Collection
- Ty Inc. Oakbrook IL, U.S.A.
- Ty UK Ltd. Fareham, Hants PO15 5TX
- Ty Deutschland 90008 Nürnberg

Handmade in China

[Beanie Name]™ [Style Number]

DATE OF BIRTH: [Month-Day-Year]

[Beanie Poem]

Visit our web page!!!
http://www.ty.com

Grunt the Razorback retired in May 1997.

Item #: 4092
Issued: 1995
Retired: 5/97
Birthday: 7/19/95

Some Beanies think Grunt is tough
No surprise, he's scary enough
But if you take him home you'll see
Grunt is the sweetest Beanie Baby!

47

Happy the Hippo (Old - Gray, New - Lavender)

1st Generation

The Beanie Babies Collection

[Beanie Name]™ [Style Number]

© 1993 Ty Inc. Oakbrook, IL USA
All Rights Reserved. Caution:
Remove this tag before giving
toy to a child. For ages 5 and up.
Handmade in Korea.
Surface
Wash.

2nd Generation

The Beanie Babies Collection

© 1993 Ty Inc. Oakbrook, IL. USA
All Rights Reserved. Caution:
Remove this tag before giving
toy to a child. For ages 3 and up.
Handmade in China.
Surface
Wash.

[Beanie Name]™ [Style Number]

to _____

from _____

with
love

3rd Generation

The Beanie Babies™ Collection

© Ty Inc.
Oakbrook IL. U.S.A.

© Ty UK Ltd.
Waterlooville, Hants
PO8 8HH

© Ty Deutschland
90008 Nürnberg

Handmade in China

[Beanie Name]™ [Style Number]

to _____

from _____

with
love

4th Generation

The Beanie Babies™ Collection

© Ty Inc.
Oakbrook IL. U.S.A.

© Ty UK Ltd.
Fareham, Hants
PO15 5TX

© Ty Deutschland
90008 Nürnberg

Handmade in China

[Beanie Name]™ [Style Number]

DATE OF BIRTH: [Month-Day-Year]

[Beanie Poem]

Visit our web page!!!
http://www.ty.com

5th Generation

The Beanie Babies Collection

© Ty Inc.
Oakbrook, IL. U.S.A.
Ty Europe Ltd.
Fareham, Hants
PO15 5TX
Ty Canada
Aurora, Ontario
Handmade in China

[Beanie Name]™

DATE OF BIRTH: [Month-Day-Year]

[Beanie Poem]

www.ty.com

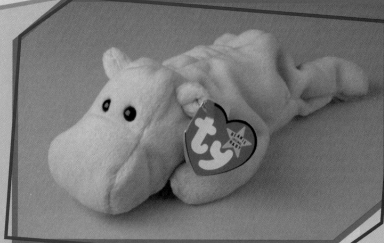

Happy was introduced in gray, a version that is now considered rare.

Item #: 4061

Issued: 1994

Birthday: 2/25/94

Happy the hippo loves to wade
In the river and in the shade
When Happy shoots water out of his snout
You know he's happy without a doubt!

48

Hippity the Mint Bunny

Hippity, like Hoppity and Floppity, is a favorite Easter gift for Beanie collectors.

Item #: 4119
Issued: 1997
Birthday: 6/1/96

Hippity is a cute little bunny
Dressed in green, he looks quite funny
Twitching his nose in the air
Sniffing a flower here and there!

Hissy the Snake

5th Generation

Hissy, unlike 1996 retiree Slither, sports a dangerous coil.

Issued: 1/98
Birthday: 4/4/97

Curled and coiled and ready to play
He waits for you patiently every day
He'll keep his best friend, but not his skin
And stay with you through thick and thin!

Hoot the Owl

Hoot the Owl was retired in October 1997.

Item #: 4073
Issued: 1995
Retired: 10/97
Birthday: 8/9/95

Late to bed, late to rise
Nevertheless, Hoot's quite wise
Studies by candlelight, nothing new
Like a president, do you know who?

51

Hoppity the Pink Bunny

Hoppity, like Hippity and Floppity, is a favorite Easter gift for Beanie collectors.

Item #: 4117

Issued: 1997

Birthday: 4/3/96

Hopscotch is what she likes to play
If you don't join in, she'll hop away
So play a game if you have the time
She likes to play, rain or shine.

Humphrey the Camel

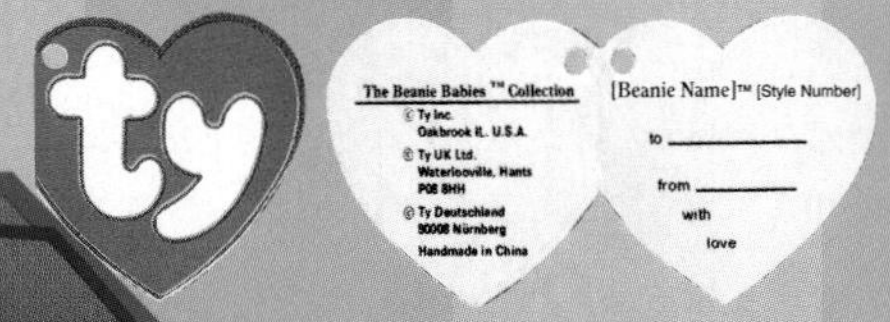

1st Generation

2nd Generation

3rd Generation

Humphrey the Camel was retired in spring 1996.

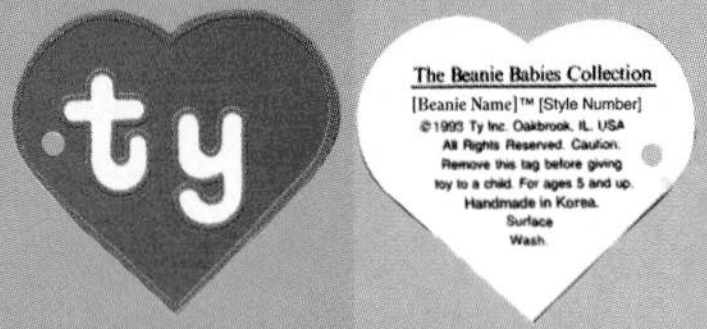

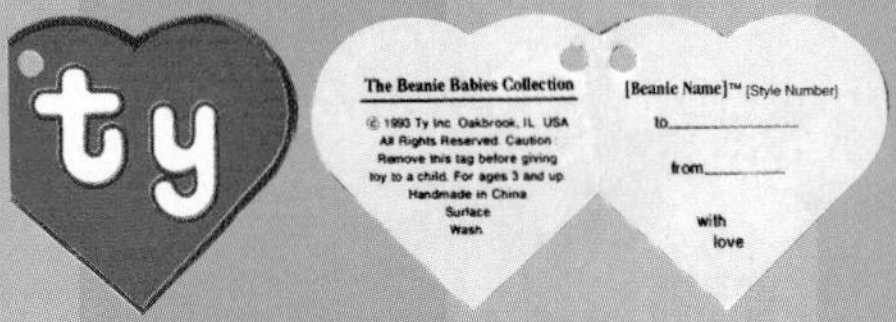

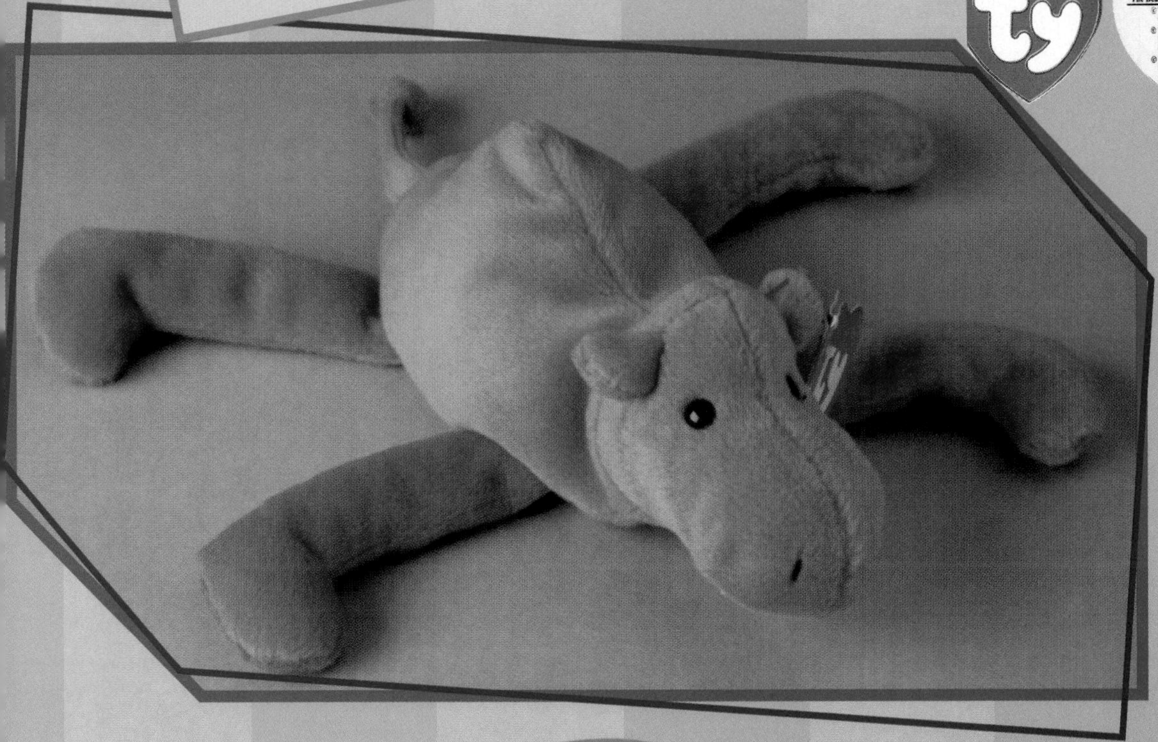

Poem: None

Item #: 4060

Issued: 1994

Retired: 1996

Birthday: Unknown

Iggy the Iguana

5th Generation

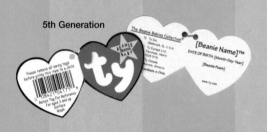

Iggy's coloring reminds many of Sting the Ray and Bronty the Brontosaurus.

Issued: 1/98
Birthday: 8/12/97

Sitting on a rock, basking in the sun
Is this Iguana's idea of fun
Towel and glasses, book and beach chair
His life is so perfect without a care!

Inch the Worm

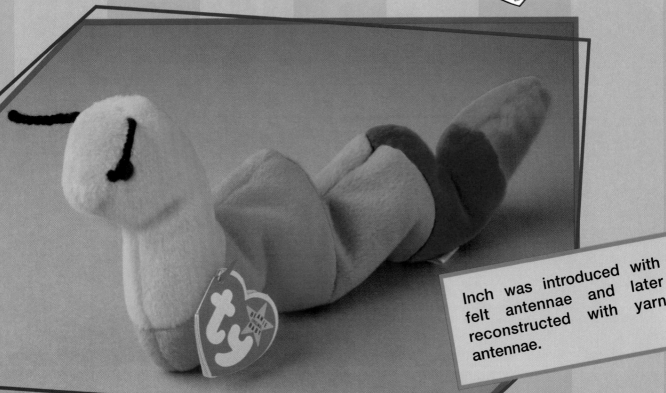

Inch was introduced with felt antennae and later reconstructed with yarn antennae.

Item #: 4044
Issued: 1995
Birthday: 9/3/95

Inch the worm is a friend of mine
He goes so slow all the time
Inching around from here to there
Traveling the world without a care.

Inky the Octopus (Old - Tan, New - Pink)

1st Generation

The Beanie Babies Collection
[Beanie Name]™ [Style Number]
© 1993 Ty Inc. Oakbrook, IL USA
All Rights Reserved. Caution:
Remove this tag before giving
toy to a child. For ages 5 and up.
Handmade in Korea.
Surface
Wash

2nd Generation

The Beanie Babies Collection
© 1993 Ty Inc. Oakbrook, IL. USA
All Rights Reserved. Caution:
Remove this tag before giving
toy to a child. For ages 3 and up.
Handmade in China
Surface
Wash

[Beanie Name]™ [Style Number]
to _____
from _____
with
love

3rd Generation

The Beanie Babies ™ Collection
© Ty Inc.
Oakbrook IL, U.S.A.
© Ty UK Ltd.
Waterlooville, Hants
P08 8KH
Handmade in China

[Beanie Name]™ [Style Number]
to _____
from _____
with
love

4th Generation

The Beanie Babies™ Collection
© Ty Inc.
Oakbrook IL, U.S.A.
© Ty UK Ltd.
Fareham, Hants
P015 5TX
© Ty Deutschland
90008 Nürnberg
Handmade in China

[Beanie Name]™ [Style Number]
DATE OF BIRTH : [Month-Day-Year]
[Beanie Poem]
Visit our web page!!!
http://www.ty.com

5th Generation

The Beanie Babies Collection™
© Ty Inc.
Oakbrook, IL, U.S.A.
© Ty Europe Ltd
Fareham, Hants
P015 5TX
Ty Canada
Aurora, Ontario
Handmade in China

[Beanie Name]™
DATE OF BIRTH: [Month-Day-Year]
[Beanie Poem]
www.ty.com

The first Inky was tan without a mouth. Later the mouth was added. The last version of Inky is the pink version.

Item #: 4028
Issued: 1994
Birthday: 11/29/94

Inky's head is big and round
As he swims he makes no sound
If you need a hand, don't hesitate
Inky can help because he has eight!

Jolly the Walrus

Jolly, who made his debut in May 1997, is the replacement for the January 1997 retiree Tusk the Walrus. Jolly sports long-haired plush whiskers and filled felt tusks that give him a more realistic appearance.

Item #: 4082

Issued: 1997

Birthday: 12/2/96

Jolly the walrus is not very serious
He laughs and laughs until he's delirious
He often reminds me of my dad
Always happy, never sad!

Kiwi the Toucan

Kiwi was retired in May 1997.

Item #: 4070
Issued: 1995
Retired: 5/97
Birthday: 9/16/95

Kiwi waits for April showers
Watching a garden bloom with flowers
There trees grow with fruit that's sweet
I'm sure you'll guess his favorite treat!

58

Lefty the Donkey

4th Generation

Lefty was introduced to mark the 1996 election year. He was retired in January 1997.

Item #: 4057
Issued: 1996
Retired: 1/97
Birthday: 7/4/96

Donkeys to the left, elephants to the right
Often seems like a crazy sight
This whole game seems very funny
Until you realize they're spending your money!

Legs the Frog

1st Generation

2nd Generation

3rd Generation

4th Generation

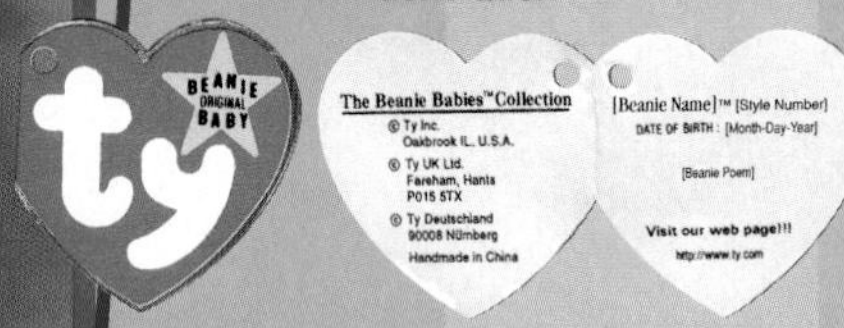

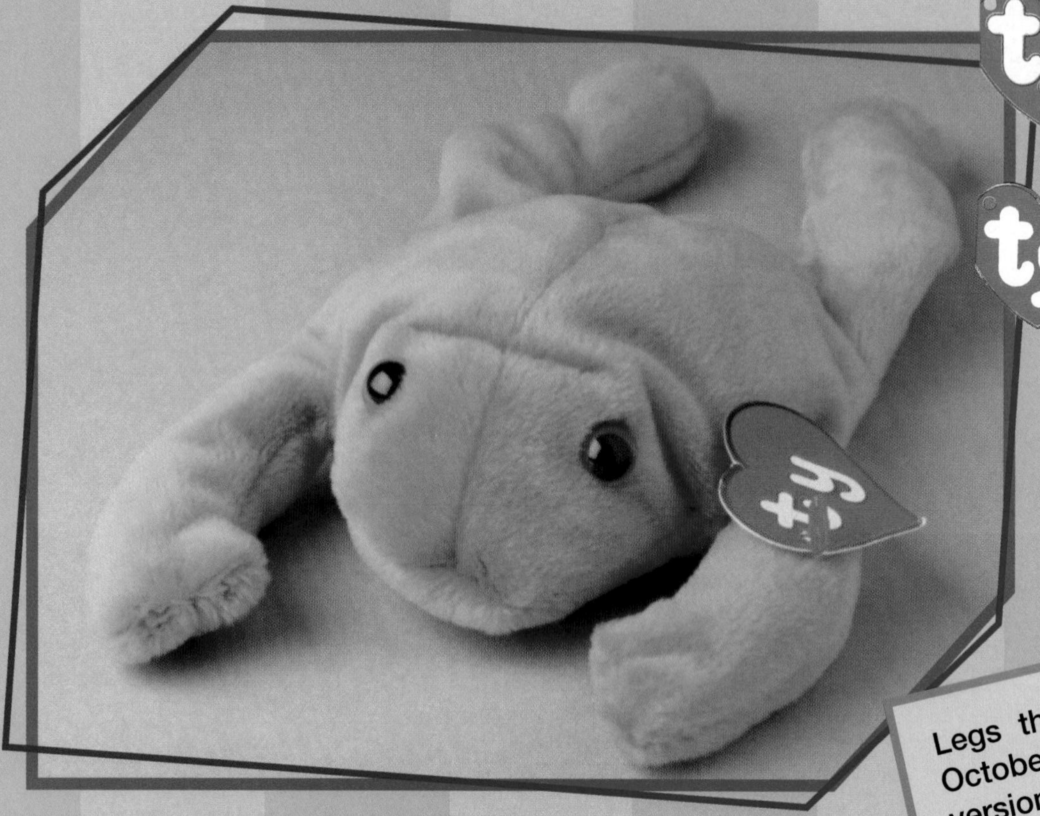

Legs the Frog was retired in October 1997. In the old-tag versions, he was plumper and his eyes were spread out a little more. The older Legs also had more well-defined hands.

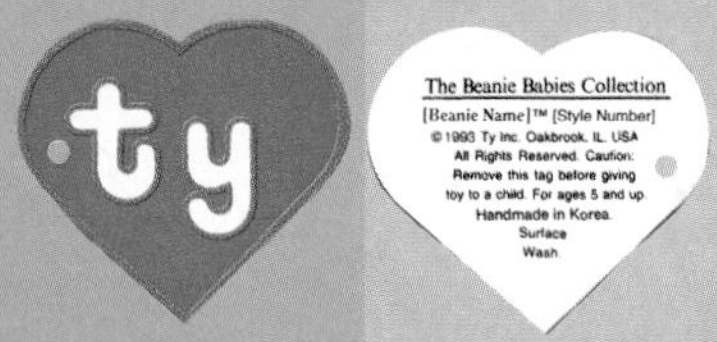

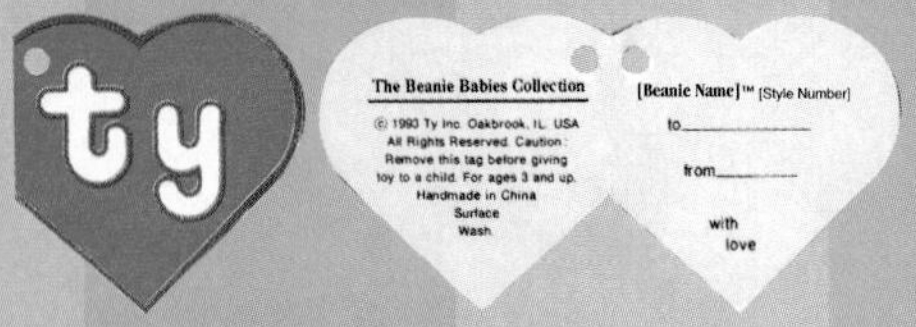

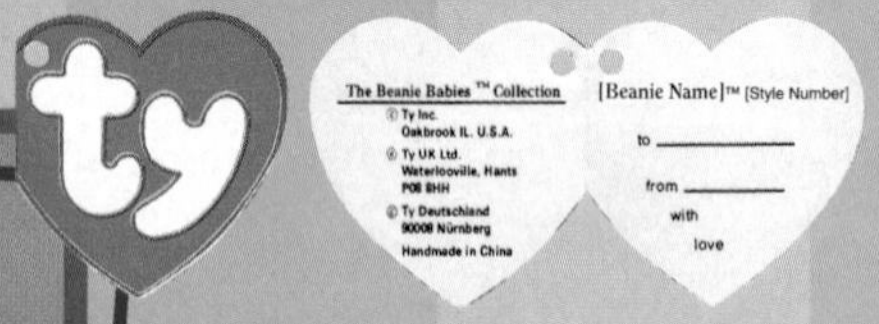

Item #: 4020
Issued: 1994
Retired: 10/97
Birthday: 4/25/93

Legs lives in a hollow log
Legs likes to play leap frog
If you like to hang out at the lake
Legs will be the new friend you make!

Libearty the Bear

4th Generation

The Beanie Babies™ Collection
℗ Ty Inc.
Oakbrook IL., U.S.A.
℗ Ty UK Ltd.
Fareham, Hants
PO15 5TX
℗ Ty Deutschland
90008 Nürnberg
Handmade in China

[Beanie Name]™ [Style Number]
DATE OF BIRTH [Month-Day-Year]

[Beanie Poem]

Visit our web page!!!
http://www.ty.com

Libearty was intro-
duced in 1996 to mark
the Olympic Games in
Atlanta. Libearty is the
only Beanie to have
a vague birthday of a
season and a year,
summer 1996. He was
retired later that year.

Item #: 4057

Issued: 1996

Retired: 1996

Birthday: Unknown

I am called Libearty
I wear the flag for all to see
Hope and freedom is my way
That's why I wear flag USA.

Lizzy

the Lizard
(Old - Tie-dyed, New - Blue & Yellow)

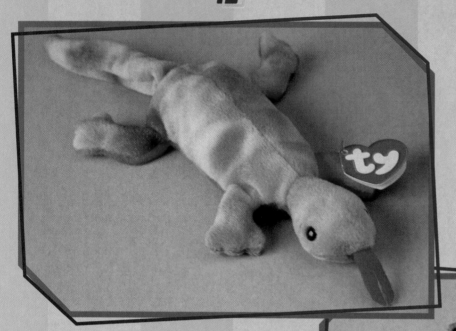

3rd Generation

4th Generation

The first issue of Lizzy was tie-dyed. It was then redesigned as the Lizzy we see today. She retired in January 1998.

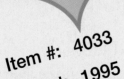

Item #: 4033
Issued: 1995
Retired: 1/98
Birthday: 5/11/95

Lizzy loves Legs the frog
She hides with him under logs
Both of them search for flies
Underneath the clear blue skies!

62

Lucky the Ladybug
(Old - 7 Glued Dots, New - Large & Small Dots)

1st Generation

The Beanie Babies Collection
[Beanie Name]™ [Style Number]
© 1993 Ty Inc. Oakbrook, IL USA
All Rights Reserved. Caution:
Remove this tag before giving
toy to a child. For ages 5 and up.
Handmade in Korea.
Surface
Wash

2nd Generation

The Beanie Babies Collection
© 1993 Ty Inc. Oakbrook, IL. USA
All Rights Reserved. Caution:
Remove this tag before giving
toy to a child. For ages 3 and up.
Handmade in China
Surface
Wash

[Beanie Name]™ [Style Number]
to _____
from _____
with
love

3rd Generation

The Beanie Babies ™ Collection
© Ty Inc.
Oakbrook IL. U.S.A.
© Ty UK Ltd.
Waterlooville, Hants
P08 8HH
© Ty Deutschland
90008 Nürnberg
Handmade in China

[Beanie Name]™ [Style Number]
to _____
from _____
with
love

4th Generation

The Beanie Babies™ Collection
© Ty Inc.
Oakbrook IL. U.S.A.
© Ty UK Ltd.
Fareham, Hants
P015 5TX
© Ty Deutschland
90008 Nürnberg
Handmade in China

[Beanie Name]™ [Style Number]
DATE OF BIRTH: [Month-Day-Year]

[Beanie Poem]

Visit our web page!!!
http://www.ty.com

5th Generation

Please remove all swing tags
before giving this item to a child

The Beanie Babies Collection
© Ty Inc.
Oakbrook, IL U.S.A.
Ty Europe Ltd
Fareham, Hants
P015 5TX
Ty Canada
Aurora, Ontario
Handmade in China

[Beanie Name]™
DATE OF BIRTH: [Month-Day-Year]

[Beanie Poem]

www.ty.com

Retain Tag for Reference
For ages 3 and up
Surface
Wash

Lucky was introduced with seven glued spots. With wear, these spots would come off, so a new technique was devised with larger dots and more space in the fabric, giving her a spot count of around seven to 10. The current pattern has smaller dots and a spot count of about 21.

Item #: 4040
Issued: 1994
Birthday: 5/1/95

Lucky the lady bug loves the lotto
"Someone must win" that's her motto
But save your dimes and even a penny
Don't spend on the lotto and you'll have many!

Magic the Dragon

In its earlier days, Magic had light-pink (almost cream) stitching in its wings and nostrils. It was later changed to a regular pink, followed by hot pink (a.k.a. dark pink). Light pink stitching is considered the rarest of the three variations. Magic retired in January 1998.

3rd Generation

The Beanie Babies™ Collection
① Ty Inc.
Oakbrook IL. U.S.A.
② Ty UK Ltd.
Waterlooville, Hants
PQ8 8HH
③ Ty Deutschland
90008 Nürnberg
Handmade in China

[Beanie Name]™ [Style Number]

to _____
from _____
with
love

4th Generation

The Beanie Babies™ Collection
① Ty Inc.
Oakbrook IL. U.S.A.
② Ty UK Ltd.
Fareham, Hants
PO15 5TX
③ Ty Deutschland
90008 Nürnberg
Handmade in China

[Beanie Name]™ [Style Number]
DATE OF BIRTH: [Month-Day-Year]

[Beanie Poem]

Visit our web page!!!
http://www.ty.com

Item #:   4088
Issued: 1995
Retired: 1/98
Birthday: 9/5/95

Magic the dragon lives in a dream
The most beautiful that you have ever seen
Through magic lands she likes to fly
Look up and watch her, way up high!

Manny the Manatee

3rd Generation

The Beanie Babies ™ Collection

Ⓣ Ty Inc.
Oakbrook IL. U.S.A.

Ⓤ Ty UK Ltd.
Waterlooville, Hants
P08 8HH

Ⓓ Ty Deutschland
90008 Nürnberg

Handmade in China

[Beanie Name]™ [Style Number]

to _____

from _____

with

love

4th Generation

The Beanie Babies™ Collection

Ⓣ Ty Inc.
Oakbrook IL. U.S.A.

Ⓤ Ty UK Ltd
Fareham, Hants
P015 5TX

Ⓓ Ty Deutschland
90008 Nürnberg

Handmade in China

[Beanie Name]™ [Style Number]
DATE OF BIRTH: [Month-Day-Year]

[Beanie Poem]

Visit our web page!!!
http://www.ty.com

Manny the Manatee retired in May 1997.

Item #: 4081
Issued: 1995
Retired: 5/97
Birthday: 6/8/95

Manny is sometimes called a sea cow
She likes to twirl and likes to bow
Manny sure is glad you bought her
Because it's so lonely underwater!

Maple the Canadian Exclusive Bear

Maple the Canadian Exclusive Bear Pride was this bear's name in development. Upon introduction, Pride's name changed to Maple. Pride tags were already sewn in, but the hang tags were changed to its official name of Maple.

Item #: 4600
Issued: 1996
Birthday: 7/1/96

Maple the bear likes to ski
With his friends, he plays hockey.
He loves his pancakes and eats every crumb
Can you guess which country he's from?

Mel the Koala Bear

4th Generation

5th Generation

Kids love Koalas, and Mel is one of the more easily obtained of the Beanies.

Item #: 4162
Issued: 1997
Birthday: 1/15/96

How do you name a Koala bear?
It's rather tough, I do declare!
It confuses me, I get in a funk
I'll name him Mel, after my favorite hunk!

Mystic the Unicorn

1st Generation

2nd Generation

3rd Generation

4th Generation

5th Generation

Like Derby the Horse, Mystic also had its mane altered. It was introduced with the fine yarn and was then changed to the coarse yarn. An iridescent horn recently replaced the old solid-colored horn.

Item #: 4007

Issued: 1994

Birthday: 5/21/94

Once upon a time so far away
A unicorn was born one day in May
Keep Mystic with you, she's a prize
You'll see the magic in her blue eyes!

Nanook the Husky

4th Generation

5th Generation

Nanook has been a little harder to find than many of the other dogs in the collection.

Item #: 4104

Issued: 1997

Birthday: 11/21/96

Nanook is a dog that loves cold weather
To him a sled is light as a feather
Over the snow and through the slush
He runs at hearing the cry of "mush!"

Nip

the Gold Cat (Old - Gold with White Face & Belly [top left], Old - All Gold [top right], New - Gold with White Paws)

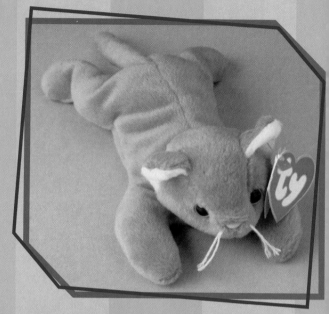

2nd Generation

The Beanie Babies Collection
© 1993 Ty Inc. Oakbrook, IL, USA
All Rights Reserved. Caution
Remove this tag before giving
toy to a child. For ages 3 and up.
Handmade in China
Surface
Wash.

[Beanie Name]™ [Style Number]
to _____
from _____
with
love

3rd Generation

The Beanie Babies ™ Collection
© Ty Inc.
Oakbrook IL, U.S.A.
© Ty UK Ltd.
Waterlooville, Hants
P08 BHH
© Ty Deutschland
90008 Nürnberg
Handmade in China

[Beanie Name]™ [Style Number]
to _____
from _____
with
love

4th Generation

The Beanie Babies™ Collection
© Ty Inc.
Oakbrook IL, U.S.A.
© Ty UK Ltd.
Fareham, Hants
P015 STX
© Ty Deutschland
90008 Nürnberg
Handmade in China

[Beanie Name]™ [Style Number]
DATE OF BIRTH : [Month-Day-Year]

[Beanie Poem]

Visit our web page!!!
http://www.ty.com

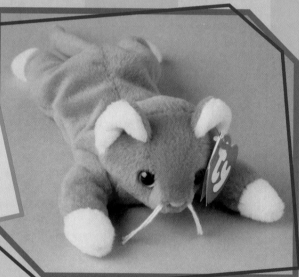

So far this cat has had three lives. She has been all gold, gold with a white face and belly, and gold with white paws. Nip retired in January 1998.

Item #:   4003

Issued: 1994

Retired: 1/98

Birthday: 3/6/94

His name is Nipper, but we call him Nip
His best friend is a black cat named Zip
Nip likes to run in races for fun
He runs so fast he's always number one!

Nuts the Squirrel

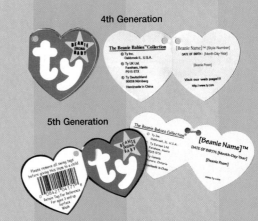

4th Generation

5th Generation

Nuts was introduced in the New Year's 1997 announce-ments. Thanks to Nuts' tail, he is the first Beanie to have long-haired plush on its body.

Item #: 4114

Issued: 1997

Birthday: 1/21/96

With his bushy tail, he'll scamper up a tree
The most cheerful critter you'll ever see.
He's nuts about nuts, and he loves to chat
Have you ever seen a squirrel like that?

Patti the Platypus (Old - Maroon, New - Purple)

1st Generation

The Beanie Babies Collection
[Beanie Name]™ [Style Number]
© 1993 Ty Inc. Oakbrook, IL. USA
All Rights Reserved. Caution:
Remove this tag before giving
toy to a child. For ages 5 and up.
Handmade in Korea.
Surface
Wash

2nd Generation

The Beanie Babies Collection
[Beanie Name]™ [Style Number]
© 1993 Ty Inc. Oakbrook, IL. USA
All Rights Reserved. Caution:
Remove this tag before giving
toy to a child. For ages 3 and up.
Handmade in China
Surface
Wash

to _____
from _____
with love

3rd Generation

ty

The Beanie Babies ™ Collection
© Ty Inc.
Oakbrook IL. U.S.A.
Ty UK Ltd.
Waterlooville, Hants
PO8 2HH
Ty Deutschland
90008 Nürnberg
Handmade in China

[Beanie Name]™ [Style Number]
to _____
from _____
with love

4th Generation
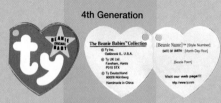

The Beanie Babies™ Collection
© Ty Inc.
Oakbrook, IL, U.S.A.
Ty UK Ltd.
Fareham, Hants
PO15 5TX
Ty Deutschland
90008 Nürnberg
Handmade in China

[Beanie Name]™ [Style Number]
DATE OF BIRTH: [Month-Day-Year]
[Beanie Poem]
Visit our web page!!!
http://www.ty.com

5th Generation

The Beanie Babies Collection
© Ty Inc.
Oakbrook, IL. U.S.A.
Ty Europe Ltd.
Fareham, Hants
PO15 5TX
Ty Canada
Aurora, Ontario
Handmade in China

[Beanie Name]™
DATE OF BIRTH: [Month-Day-Year]
[Beanie Poem]
www.Ty.com

Please remove all swing tags
before giving this item to a child

> One of the original nine, Patti was originally a maroon color but shortly thereafter changed to the magenta Patti we see today. There are very few maroon Pattis, which are quite expensive.

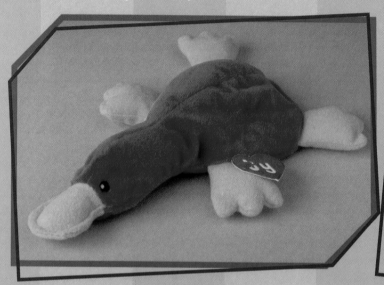

Item #: 4025
Issued: 1994
Birthday: 1/6/93

Ran into Patti one day while walking
Believe me she wouldn't stop talking!
Listened and listened to her speak
That would explain her extra large beak!

Peace the Tie-dye Bear

4th Generation

5th Generation

When Garcia was retired in May 1997, Peace the tie-dyed bear made its appearance on the Ty Inc. website.

Item #: 4053
Issued: 1997
Birthday: 2/1/96

All races all colors, under the sun
Join hands together and have some fun
Dance to the music, rock and roll is the sound
Symbols of peace and love abound!

73

Peanut the Elephant
(Old - Royal Blue, New - Light Blue)

3rd Generation

4th Generation

5th Generation

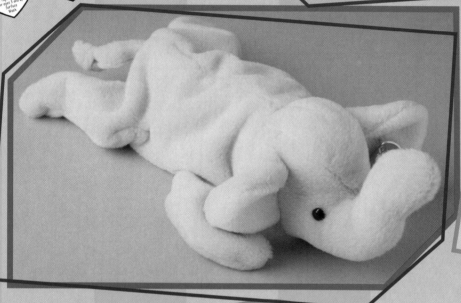

When Peanut was first introduced, he was bright cobalt blue, which is now known as the "Dark Blue Peanut" to collectors. Peanut was then reconstructed with the current light blue that we see today.

Item #: 4062

Issued: 1995

Birthday: 1/25/95

Peanut the elephant walks on tip-toes
Quietly sneaking wherever she goes
She'll sneak up on you and a hug you will get
Peanuts is a friend you won't soon forget.

Peking the Panda Bear

1st Generation

The Beanie Babies Collection

[Beanie Name]™ [Style Number]
© 1993 Ty Inc. Oakbrook, IL. USA
All Rights Reserved. Caution:
Remove this tag before giving
toy to a child. For ages 5 and up.
Handmade in Korea.
Surface
Wash.

2nd Generation

The Beanie Babies Collection

© 1993 Ty Inc. Oakbrook, IL. USA
All Rights Reserved. Caution:
Remove this tag before giving
toy to a child. For ages 3 and up.
Handmade in China.
Surface
Wash.

[Beanie Name]™ [Style Number]

to _____
from _____
with
love

3rd Generation

The Beanie Babies ™ Collection

© Ty Inc.
Oakbrook II. U.S.A.

© Ty UK Ltd.
Waterlooville, Hants
P08 BHH

© Ty Deutschland
9000K Nürnberg
Handmade in China

[Beanie Name]™ [Style Number]

to _____
from _____
with
love

Peking the Panda Bear
retired in spring 1996.

Poem: None

Item #: 4013

Issued: 1994

Retired: 1996

Birthday: Unknown

75

Pinchers the Lobster

Pinchers has donned all five generations of tags.

1st Generation

2nd Generation

3rd Generation

4th Generation

5th Generation

Item #: 4026
Issued: 1994
Birthday: 6/19/93

This lobster loves to pinch
Eating his food inch by inch
Balancing carefully with his tail
Moving forward slow as a snail!

Pinky the Flamingo

3rd Generation

4th Generation

5th Generation

Pinky's Teenie Beanie counterpart was the hottest McDonald's give-away of 1997.

Item #: 4072
Issued: 1995
Birthday: 2/13/95

Pinky loves the Everglades
From the hottest pink she's made
With floppy legs and big orange beak
She's the Beanie that you seek!

Pouch the Kangaroo

Pouch was introduced in January 1997 and holds the title of being the only Beanie Baby that included another baby — her joey.

Item #: 4161
Issued: 1997
Birthday: 11/6/96

My little pouch is handy I've found
It helps me carry my baby around
I hop up and down without any fear
Knowing my baby is safe and near.

78

Pounce the Cat

5th Generation

Pounce was introduced in January 1998. He is dark brown with white highlights.

Issued: 1/98
Birthday: 8/28/97

Sneaking and slinking down the hall
To pounce upon a fluffy yarn ball
Under the tables, around the chairs
Through the rooms and down the stairs!

79

Prance the Cat

5th Generation

Prance was introduced in January 1998. He is a gray tabby with black stripes and white high-lights.

Issued: 1/98
Birthday: 11/20/97

She darts around and swats the air
Then looks confused when nothing's there
Pick her up and pet her soft fur
Listen closely, and you'll hear her purr!

Princess Bear

Introduced in 1997 to benefit the Diana, Princess of Wales, fund, Princess was a huge hit. Concerns about her initial availability eased as more shipments arrived in stores for 1998.

Item #: n/a

Issued: 1997

Birthday: n/a

Like an angel, she came from heaven above
She shared her compassion, her pain, her love
She only stayed with us long enough to teach
The world to share, to give, to reach.

Puffer the Puffin

5th Generation

No, it's not a penguin! Puffer the Puffin introduced collectors to a new species in 1998.

Issued: 1/98
Birthday: 11/3/97

What in the world does a puffin do?
We're sure that you would like to know too
We asked Puffer how she spends her days
Before she answered, she flew away!

Pugsly the Pug Dog

Although not as tough as Nanook, Pugsly is slightly tougher than other dogs.

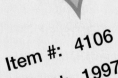

Item #: 4106
Issued: 1997
Birthday: 5/2/96

Pugsly is picky about what he will wear
Never a spot, a stain or a tear
Image is something of which he'll gloat
Until he noticed his wrinkled coat!

Quackers the Duck
(Old - Without Wings, New - With Wings)

1st Generation

The Beanie Babies Collection
[Beanie Name]™ [Style Number]
© 1993 Ty Inc. Oakbrook, IL. USA
All Rights Reserved. Caution:
Remove this tag before giving
toy to a child. For ages 5 and up.
Handmade in Korea.
Surface.
Wash.

2nd Generation

The Beanie Babies Collection

[Beanie Name]™ [Style Number]

© 1993 Ty Inc. Oakbrook, IL. USA
All Rights Reserved. Caution:
Remove this tag before giving
toy to a child. For ages 3 and up.
Handmade in China.
Surface.
Wash.

to _____
from _____
with
love

3rd Generation

The Beanie Babies ™ Collection

[Beanie Name]™ [Style Number]

① Ty Inc.
Oakbrook IL. U.S.A.
② Ty UK Ltd.
Waterlooville, Hants
PO8 8KH
③ Ty Deutschland
90008 Nürnberg
Handmade in China

to _____
from _____
with
love

4th Generation

The Beanie Babies™ Collection

[Beanie Name]™ [Style Number]

① Ty Inc.
Oakbrook IL... U.S.A.
② Ty UK Ltd.
Fareham, Hants
PO15 5TX
③ Ty Deutschland
90008 Nürnberg
Handmade in China

DATE OF BIRTH: [Month-Day-Year]

[Beanie Poem]

Visit our web page!!!
http://www.ty.com

5th Generation

The Beanie Babies Collection ™

[Beanie Name]™

① Ty Inc.
Oakbrook, IL. U.S.A.
Ty Europe Ltd.
Fareham, Hants
PO15 5TX
Ty Canada
Aurora, Ontario
Handmade in China

DATE OF BIRTH: [Month-Day-Year]

[Beanie Poem]

www.ty.com

Please remove all swing tags
before giving this item to a child

Retain Tag For Reference
For ages 3 and up
Surface
Wash

> Quackers debuted without wings! Very few of these Quackers exist, as it was quickly reconstructed with wings.

Item #: 4024
Issued: 1994
Birthday: 4/19/94

There is a duck by the name of Quackers
Every night he eats animal crackers
He swims in a lake that's clear and blue
But he'll come to the shore to be with you!

84

Radar the Bat

3rd Generation

4th Generation

On January 29, 1997, Ty made an announcement to all its representatives that Sparky and Radar were retired. Stores were bombarded with requests for the two retired Beanies, prompting Ty to reconsider the next day. Radar's retirement became effective again in May 1997.

Item #: 4091
Issued: 1995
Retired: 5/97
Birthday: 10/30/95

Radar the bat flies late at night
He can soar to an amazing height
If you see something as high as a star
Take a good look, it might be Radar!

Rainbow the Chameleon

With Iggy, Rainbow was the second reptilian addition to the line in January 1998.

Issued: 1/98
Birthday: 10/14/97

Red, green, blue and yellow
This chameleon is a colorful fellow
A blend of colors, his own unique hue
Rainbow was made especially for you!

Rex the Tyrannosaurus

3rd Generation

The Beanie Babies ™ Collection

① Ty Inc.
Oakbrook IL, U.S.A.

② Ty UK Ltd.
Waterlooville, Hants
PO8 8HH

③ Ty Deutschland
90008 Nürnberg

Handmade in China

[Beanie Name]™ [Style Number]

to _____
from _____
with
love

Since Tyrannosaurus Rex has always been the most popular dinosaur, it was no surprise that Rex would be just as popular. Although he is not as rare as Bronty the Brontosaurus, he is the most sought after dinosaur in the trio. Rex was retired with Bronty and Steg in spring 1996.

Poem: None

Item #: 4086

Issued: 1995

Retired: 1996

Birthday: Unknown

Righty the Elephant

4th Generation

To mark the 1996 Presidential election, Lefty and Righty were introduced and summarily retired in January 1997.

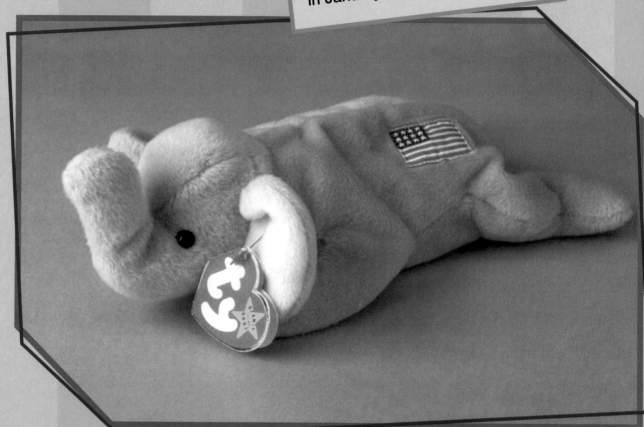

Item #: 4086
Issued: 1996
Retired: 1/97
Birthday: 7/4/96

Donkeys to the left, elephants to the right
Often seems like a crazy sight
This whole game seems very funny
Until you realize they're spending your money!

Ringo the Raccoon

The "old tag" Ringo is significantly more expensive than the new tag.

3rd Generation

The Beanie Babies™ Collection

① Ty Inc.
Oakbrook IL, U.S.A.

② Ty UK Ltd.
Waterlooville, Hants
PO8 8HH

③ Ty Deutschland
90008 Nürnberg

Handmade in China

[Beanie Name]™ [Style Number]

to _____

from _____

with

love

4th Generation

The Beanie Babies™ Collection

① Ty Inc.
Oakbrook IL, U.S.A.

② Ty UK Ltd.
Fareham, Hants
PO15 5TX

③ Ty Deutschland
90008 Nürnberg

Handmade in China

[Beanie Name]™ [Style Number]

DATE OF BIRTH: [Month-Day-Year]

[Beanie Poem]

Visit our web page!!!
http://www.ty.com

5th Generation

The Beanie Babies Collection

① Ty Inc.
Oakbrook, IL. U.S.A.

② Ty Europe Ltd.
Fareham, Hants
PO15 5TX

③ Ty Canada
Aurora, Ontario

Handmade in China

[Beanie Name]™

DATE OF BIRTH: [Month-Day-Year]

[Beanie Poem]

www.ty.com

Please remove all swing tags
before giving this item to a child

Return Tag For Reference
For ages 3 and up
Surface
Wash

Item #: 4014

Issued: 1995

Birthday: 7/14/95

Ringo hides behind his mask
He will come out, if you should ask
He loves to chitter, he loves to chatter
Just about anything, it doesn't matter!

Roary the Lion

4th Generation

The Beanie Babies™ Collection

© Ty Inc.
Oakbrook IL. U.S.A.

® Ty UK Ltd.
Fareham, Hants
PO15 5TX

® Ty Deutschland
90008 Nürnberg

Handmade in China

[Beanie Name]™ [Style Number]

DATE OF BIRTH: [Month-Day-Year]

[Beanie Poem]

Visit our web page!!!
http://www.ty.com

5th Generation

The Beanie Babies Collection

© Ty Inc.
Oakbrook, IL, U.S.A.
Ty Europe Ltd.
Fareham, Hants
PO15 5TX
Ty Canada
Aurora, Ontario
Handmade in China

Please remove all swing tags
before giving this item to a child

Reban Toy For Reference
For ages 3 and up
Surface
Wash

[Beanie Name]

DATE OF BIRTH: [Month-Day-Yr]

[Beanie Poem]

www.ty.com

Breaking with tradition in keeping new Beanie Babies secret before their debuts, Roary had a guest appearance with the vice president of Ty Inc. on the "Today Show."

Item #:   4069
Issued: 1997
Birthday: 2/20/96

Deep in the jungle they crowned him king
But being brave is not his thing
A cowardly lion some may say
He hears his roar and runs away!

Rover the Red Dog

4th Generation

The Beanie Babies™ Collection

© Ty Inc.
Oakbrook IL, U.S.A.
© Ty UK Ltd.
Fareham, Hants
PO15 5TX
© Ty Deutschland
90008 Nürnberg
Handmade in China

[Beanie Name]™ [Style Number]
DATE OF BIRTH: [Month-Day-Year]
[Beanie Poem]
Visit our web page!!!
http://www.ty.com

5th Generation

The Beanie Babies Collection™

© Ty Inc.
Oakbrook IL, U.S.A.
Ty Europe Ltd.
Fareham, Hants
PO15 5TX
Ty Canada
Aurora, Ontario
Handmade in China

Please remove all swing tag
before giving this item to a Child

Retain Tag For Reference
For ages 3 and up Surface
Wash

[Beanie Name]™
DATE OF BIRTH: [Month-Day-Year]
[Beanie Poem]
http://www.ty.com

Rover is one of the easiest-to-find dogs.

Item #: 4101
Issued: 1996
Birthday: 5/30/96

This dog is red and his name is Rover
If you call him he is sure to come over
He barks and plays with all his might
But worry not, he won't bite!

Scoop the Pelican

4th Generation

5th Generation

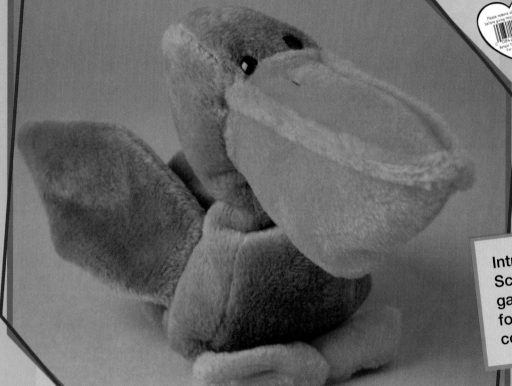

Introduced in 1996, Scoop has never gained much of a following among collectors.

Item #: 4107
Issued: 1996
Birthday: 7/1/96

All day long he scoops up fish
To fill his bill, is his wish
Diving fast and diving low
Hoping those fish are very slow

Scottie the Black Terrier

In spring 1996, Scottie (along with Curly) became one of the first napped Beanie Babies in the collection.

Item #: 4102

Issued: 1996

Birthday: 6/15/96

Scottie is a friendly sort
Even though his legs are short
He is always happy as can be
His best friends are you and me!

Seamore the White Seal

1st Generation

The Beanie Babies Collection
[Beanie Name] [Style Number]
© 1993 Ty Inc. Oakbrook, IL, USA
All Rights Reserved. Caution:
Remove this tag before giving
toy to a child. For ages 5 and up.
Handmade in Korea.
Surface
Wash.

2nd Generation

The Beanie Babies Collection
[Beanie Name] [Style Number]
© 1993 Ty Inc. Oakbrook, IL, USA
All Rights Reserved. Caution:
Remove this tag before giving
toy to a child. For ages 3 and up.
Handmade in China
Surface
Wash.

to _____
from _____
with
love

3rd Generation

The Beanie Babies ™ Collection
[Beanie Name]™ [Style Number]
© Ty Inc.
Oakbrook IL. U.S.A.
© Ty UK Ltd.
Waterlooville, Hants
P08 8HH
© Ty Deutschland
90008 Nürnberg
Handmade in China

to _____
from _____
with
love

4th Generation

The Beanie Babies™Collection
[Beanie Name]™ [Style Number]
© Ty Inc.
Oakbrook IL. U.S.A.
© Ty UK Ltd.
Fareham, Hants
PO15 5TX
© Ty Deutschland
90008 Nürnberg
Handmade in China

DATE OF BIRTH: [Month-Day-Year]

[Beanie Poem]

Visit our web page!!!
http://www.ty.com

Seamore the White
Seal was retired in
October 1997.

Item #: 4029
Issued: 1995
Retired: 10/97
Birthday: 12/14/96

Seamore is a little white seal
Fish and clams are her favorite meal
Playing and laughing in the sand
She's the happiest seal in the land!

94

Seaweed the Otter

Seaweed with a third-generation tag is quite a find. Its current tag version is more common.

Item #: 4080

Issued: 1996

Birthday: 3/19/96

Seaweed is what she likes to eat
It's supposed to be a delicious treat
Have you tried a treat from the water?
If you haven't, maybe you "otter"!

Slither the Snake

1st Generation

The Beanie Babies Collection
[Beanie Name]™ [Style Number]
© 1993 Ty Inc. Oakbrook, IL, USA
All Rights Reserved. Caution:
Remove this tag before giving
toy to a child. For ages 5 and up.
Handmade in Korea.
Surface
Wash.

2nd Generation

The Beanie Babies Collection
© 1993 Ty Inc. Oakbrook, IL, USA
All Rights Reserved. Caution:
Remove this tag before giving
toy to a child. For ages 3 and up.
Handmade in China
Surface
Wash.

[Beanie Name]™ [Style Number]
to _____
from _____
with
love

3rd Generation

The Beanie Babies ™ Collection
© Ty Inc.
Oakbrook IL. U.S.A.
© Ty UK Ltd.
Waterlooville, Hants
PO8 8HH
© Ty Deutschland
90008 Nürnberg
Handmade in China

[Beanie Name]™ [Style Number]
to _____
from _____
with
love

Slither the Snake was retired in spring 1996.

Poem: None

Item #: 4031
Issued: 1994
Retired: 1996
Birthday: Unknown

Sly the Fox

4th Generation

5th Generation

Introduced in spring 1996, Sly originally had a brown belly. This version was short lived, as the current white belly replaced it soon afterward.

Item #: 4115
Issued: 1996
Birthday: 9/12/96

Sly is a fox and tricky is he
Please don't chase him, let him be
If you want him, just say when
He'll peek out from his den!

Smoochy the Frog

The Beanie Babies Collection™

ty

BEANIE BABY

Please remove all swing tags before giving this item to a child

[Beanie Name]™
DATE OF BIRTH: [Month-Day-Year]
[Beanie Poem]

www.ty.com

© Ty Inc.
Oakbrook IL U.S.A
Ty Europe Ltd.
Fareham, Hants
PO15 5TX
Ty Canada
Aurora, Ontario
Handmade in China

Smoochy replaced 1997 retiree Legs as the amphibian representative in the collection.

Issued: 1/98
Birthday: 10/1/97

Is he a frog or maybe a prince?
This confusion makes him wince
Find the answer, help him with this
Be the one to give him a kiss!

98

Snip the Siamese Cat

Snip, although common, is a must-have for cat lovers.

Item #: 4120

Issued: 1997

Birthday: 10/22/96

Snip the cat is Siamese
She'll be your friend if you please
So toss her a toy or a piece of string
Playing with you is her favorite thing.

Snort the Bull

Snort and Tabasco have the same model number, birthday and poem. It's not a mistake: Snort is Tabasco's replacement. The only difference between the two is that Snort has white paws.

Item #: 4002
Issued: 1996
Birthday: 5/15/95

Although Snort is not so tall
He loves to play basketball
He is a star player in his dreams
Can you guess his favorite team?

Snowball the Snowman

4th Generation

Snowball's short life — introduced in October 1997, retired in January 1998 — surprised many collectors.

Item #: 4201

Issued: 1997

Retired: 1/98

Birthday: 12/22/96

There is a snowman, I've been told
That plays with Beanies out in the cold
What is better in a winter wonderland
Than a Beanie snowman in your hand!

Sparky the Dalmatian

4th Generation

The Beanie Babies™ Collection

Ⓡ Ty Inc.
Oakbrook IL. U.S.A.

Ⓡ Ty UK Ltd.
Fenham, Hants
PO15 5TX

Ⓡ Ty Deutschland
90008 Nürnberg
Handmade in China

[Beanie Name]™ [Style Number]
DATE OF BIRTH [Month-Day-Year]

[Beanie Poem]

Visit our web page!!!
http://www.ty.com

Sparky was officially retired in May 1997 to make way for its replacement — Dotty the Dalmatian. The secret of Dotty's debut was spoiled by the fact that Sparky began appearing in stores with Dotty tush tags.

Item #: 4100
Issued: 1996
Retired: 5/97
Birthday: 2/27/96

Sparky rides proud on the firetruck
Ringing the bell and pushing his luck
He gets underfoot when trying to help
He often gets stepped on and
Lets out a yelp!

Speedy the Turtle

Speedy the Turtle was retired in October 1997.

Item #: 4030
Issued: 1994
Retired: 10/97
Birthday: 8/14/94

Speedy ran marathons in the past
Such a shame, always last
Now Speedy is a big star
After he bought a racing car.

Spike the Rhinoceros

4th Generation

The Beanie Babies™ Collection
© Ty Inc.
Oakbrook IL, U.S.A.
© Ty UK Ltd.
Fareham, Hants
PO15 5TX
© Ty Deutschland
90005 Nürnberg
Handmade in China

[Beanie Name]™ [Style Number]
DATE OF BIRTH: [Month-Day-Year]

[Beanie Poem]

Visit our web page!!!
http://www.ty.com

5th Generation

The Beanie Babies Collection
© Ty Inc.
Oakbrook, IL U.S.A.
Ty Europe Ltd
Fareham, Hants
PO15 5TX
Ty Canada
Aurora, Ontario
Handmade in China

Please remove all swing tags
before giving this item to a child
Return Tag For Reference
For ages 3 and up
Surface
Wash

[Beanie Name]™
DATE OF BIRTH: [Month-Day-Year]

[Beanie Poem]

www.ty.com

Spike is a favorite Beanie of many boys.

Item #: 4060
Issued: 1996
Birthday: 8/13/96

Spike the rhino likes to stampede
He's the bruiser that you need
Gentle to birds on his back and spike
You can be his friend if you like!

Spinner the Spider

4th Generation

The Beanie Babies™ Collection

© Ty Inc.
Oakbrook IL, U.S.A.
® Ty UK Ltd.
Fareham, Hants
PO15 5TX
® Ty Deutschland
90008 Nürnberg
Handmade in China

[Beanie Name]™ [Style Number]
DATE OF BIRTH: [Month-Day-Year]

[Beanie Poem]

Visit our web page!!!
http://www.ty.com

5th Generation

The Beanie Babies Collection™

© Ty Inc.
Oakbrook, IL, U.S.A.
Ty Europe Ltd.
Fareham, Hants
PO15 5TX
Ty Canada
Aurora, Ontario
Handmade in China

[Beanie Name]™
DATE OF BIRTH: [Month-Day-Year]

[Beanie Poem]

www.ty.com

Please remove all swing tags
before giving this item to a child

Action Tag For Reference
For ages 3 and up
Surface
Wash

One of the holiday introductions for 1997, Spinner has been a tough find right from the beginning.

Item #: 4036
Issued: 1997
Birthday: 10/28/96

Does this spider make you scared?
Among many people that feeling is shared
Remember spiders have feelings too
In fact, this spider really likes you!

Splash the Orca Whale

Splash the Orca Whale was retired in May 1997 to make way for Waves the Orca Whale. Splash lies flat while Waves has a pronounced curve.

1st Generation

The Beanie Babies Collection
[Beanie Name] ™ [Style Number]
© 1993 Ty Inc. Oakbrook, IL, USA
All Rights Reserved. Caution:
Remove this tag before giving
toy to a child. For ages 5 and up.
Handmade in Korea.
Surface
Wash

2nd Generation

The Beanie Babies Collection
® 1993 Ty Inc. Oakbrook, IL, USA
All Rights Reserved. Caution:
Remove this tag before giving
toy to a child. For ages 3 and up.
Handmade in China
Surface
Wash.

[Beanie Name] ™ [Style Number]
to _____
from _____
with
love

3rd Generation

The Beanie Babies ™ Collection
® Ty Inc.
Oakbrook, IL, U.S.A.
® Ty UK Ltd.
Waterlooville, Hants
PO8 8HH
® Ty Deutschland
90008 Nürnberg
Handmade in China

[Beanie Name] ™ [Style Number]
to _____
from _____
with
love

4th Generation

The Beanie Babies™ Collection
® Ty Inc.
Oakbrook IL, U.S.A.
® Ty UK Ltd.
Fareham, Hants
PO15 5TX
® Ty Deutschland
90008 Nürnberg
Handmade in China

[Beanie Name] ™ [Style Number]
DATE OF BIRTH : [Month-Day-Year]

[Beanie Poem]

Visit our web page!!!
http://www.ty.com

Item #: 4022
Issued: 1994
Retired: 5/97
Birthday: 7/8/93

Splash loves to jump and dive
He's the fastest whale alive
He always wins the 100 yard dash
With a victory jump he'll make a splash!

Spooky the Ghost

3rd Generation

The Beanie Babies ™ Collection
Ⓒ Ty Inc.
Oakbrook IL. U.S.A.
Ⓒ Ty UK Ltd.
Waterlooville, Hants
PO8 8HH
Ⓒ Ty Deutschland
90008 Nürnberg
Handmade in China

[Beanie Name]™ [Style Number]
to _____
from
with
love

4th Generation

The Beanie Babies™Collection
Ⓒ Ty Inc.
Oakbrook IL. U.S.A.
Ⓒ Ty UK Ltd.
Fenham, Hants
PO15 5TX
Ⓒ Ty Deutschland
90008 Nürnberg
Handmade in China

[Beanie Name]™ [Style Number]
DATE OF BIRTH : [Month-Day-Year]
[Beanie Poem]
Visit our web page!!!
http://www.ty.com

Spooky was first introduced as Spook. After a misprint in later tags, Spook became the current Spooky. Spooky's mouth is glued on and will sometimes come off.

Item #: 4090
Issued: 1995
Retired: 1/98
Birthday: 10/31/95

Ghosts can be a scary sight
But don't let Spooky bring you any fright
Because when you're alone, you will see
The best friend that Spooky can be!

Spot the Black and White Dog
(Old - Without Spots, New - With Spot)

1st Generation

The Beanie Babies Collection
[Beanie Name]™ [Style Number]
© 1993 Ty Inc. Oakbrook, IL, USA
All Rights Reserved. Caution:
Remove this tag before giving
toy to a child. For ages 5 and up.
Handmade in Korea.
Surface
Wash.

2nd Generation

The Beanie Babies Collection
[Beanie Name]™ [Style Number]
(C) 1993 Ty Inc. Oakbrook, IL, USA
All Rights Reserved. Caution   to_____
Remove this tag before giving
toy to a child. For ages 3 and up.   from_____
Handmade in China
Surface   with
Wash.   love

3rd Generation

The Beanie Babies ™ Collection   [Beanie Name]™ [Style Number]
© Ty Inc.
Oakbrook IL, U.S.A.   to _____
© Ty UK Ltd.
Waterlooville, Hants   from _____
P08 8HH
© Ty Deutschland   with
90008 Nürnberg   love
Handmade in China

4th Generation

The Beanie Babies™ Collection   [Beanie Name]™ [Style Number]
© Ty Inc.   DATE OF BIRTH: [Month-Day-Year]
Oakbrook IL, U.S.A.
© Ty UK Ltd.   [Beanie Poem]
Fareham, Hants
PO15 5TX   Visit our web page!!!
© Ty Deutschland   http://www.ty.com
90008 Nürnberg
Handmade in China

Spot the Black and White Dog was retired in October 1997. As one of the original nine, Spot was introduced without the black spot on its back.

Item #: 4000
Issued: 1994
Retired: 10/97
Birthday: 1/3/93

See Spot sprint, see Spot run
You and Spot will have lots of fun
Watch out now, because he's not slow
Just stand back and watch him go!

108

Spunky the Dog

5th Generation

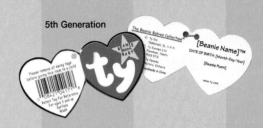

Spunky's long-haired plush ears make him a slight departure from the usual short-haired Beanies.

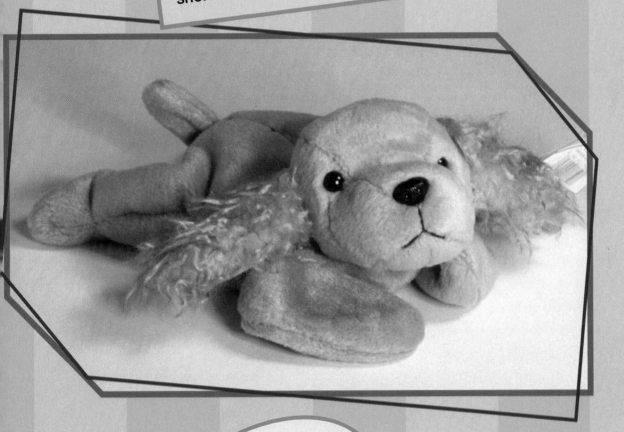

Issued: 1/98
Birthday: 1/14/97

Bouncing around without much grace
To jump on your lap and lick your face
But watch him closely, he has no fears
He'll run so fast, he'll trip over his ears!

Squealer the Pig

Squealer has worn all five generations of tags in his lifetime.

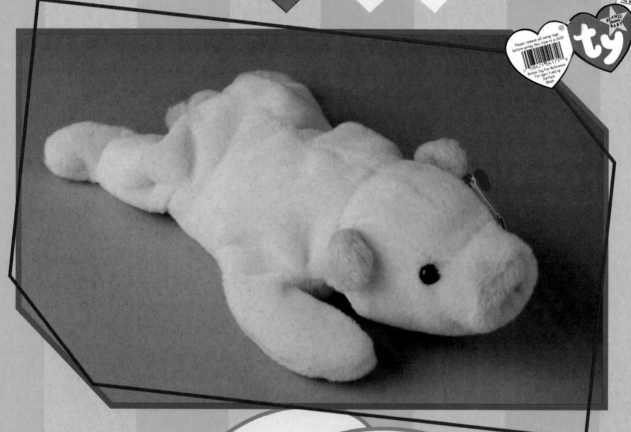

Item #: 4005
Issued: 1994
Birthday: 4/23/93

Squealer likes to joke around
He is known as class clown
Listen to his stories awhile
There is not doubt he will make you smile!

Steg
the Stegosaurus

3rd Generation

The Beanie Babies ™ Collection

© Ty Inc.
Oakbrook IL U.S.A.

© Ty UK Ltd.
Waterlooville, Hants
PO8 8HH

© Ty Deutschland
90008 Nürnberg

Handmade in China

[Beanie Name]™ [Style Number]

to _____
from _____
with
love

Steg the Stegosaurus retired in spring 1996 with Rex the Tyrannosaurus and Bronty the Brontosaurus.

Poem: None

Item #: 4087

Issued: 1995

Retired: 1996

Birthday: Unknown

111

Sting the Manta Ray

3rd Generation

The Beanie Babies™ Collection

® Ty Inc.
Oakbrook IL. U.S.A.
® Ty UK Ltd.
Waterlooville, Hants
PO8 8HH
® Ty Deutschland
90008 Nürnberg
Handmade in China

[Beanie Name]™ [Style Number]

to _____
from _____
with
love

4th Generation

The Beanie Babies™ Collection

® Ty Inc.
Oakbrook IL. U.S.A.
® Ty UK Ltd.
Fareham, Hants
PO15 5TX
® Ty Deutschland
90008 Nürnberg
Handmade in China

[Beanie Name]™ [Style Number]
DATE OF BIRTH: [Month-Day-Year]

[Beanie Poem]

Visit our web page!!!
http://www.ty.com

Sting was retired in January 1997 possibly due to defects in the stitching. In mint condition, Sting is one of the more valuable January 1997 retirees.

Item #: 4077
Issued: 1995
Retired: 1/97
Birthday: 8/27/95

I'm a manta ray and my name is Sting
I'm quite unusual and this is the thing
Under the water I glide like a bird
Have you ever seen something so absurd?

Stinky the Skunk

3rd Generation

4th Generation

5th Generation

Stinky was a big hit among skunk fans.

Item #: 4017
Issued: 1995
Birthday: 2/13/95

Deep in the woods he lived in a cave
Perfume and mints were the gifts he gave
He showered every night in the kitchen sink
Hoping one day he wouldn't stink!

Stretch the Ostrich

5th Generation

The Beanie Babies Collection

Please remove all swing tags before giving this item to a Child

Retain Tag for Reference
For ages 3 and up
Surface
Wash

ty

© Ty Inc.
Oakbrook, IL U.S.A.
Ty Europe Ltd
Fareham, Hants
PO15 5TX
Ty Canada
Aurora, Ontario
Handmade in China

BEANIE BABY

[Beanie Name]™
DATE OF BIRTH: [Month-Day-Year]

[Beanie Name]™

[Beanie Poem]

www.ty.com

Stretch's fluffy collar, like Spunky the Dog's ears, are a long-haired plush change from the usual short-hair of the Beanies line.

Issued: 1/98
Birthday: 9/21/97

She thinks when her head is underground
The rest of her body can't be found
The Beanie Babies think it's absurd
To play hide and seek with this bird!

114

Stripes

the Tiger (Old - Dark with More Stripes, New - Light with Less Stripes)

3rd Generation

The Beanie Babies ™ Collection	[Beanie Name]™ [Style Number]
® Ty Inc. Oakbrook IL USA. ® Ty UK Ltd. Waterlooville, Hants P08 8NH ® Ty Deutschland 90008 Nürnberg Handmade in China	to _____ from _____ with love

4th Generation

The Beanie Babies™ Collection	[Beanie Name]™ [Style Number] DATE OF BIRTH: [Month-Day-Year] [Beanie Poem] Visit our web page!!! http://www.ty.com
® Ty Inc. Oakbrook IL. USA. ® Ty UK Ltd. Fareham, Hants P015 5TX ® Ty Deutschland 90008 Nürnberg Handmade in China	

5th Generation

The first version of Stripes was a darker orange color with more black stripes. Stripes was changed to lighter orange and fewer stripes. Some people have found the old style stripes with a "fuzzy belly," as if the stripes were not well-defined on its belly.

Item #: 4065

Issued: 1995

Birthday: 6/11/95

Stripes was never fierce nor strong
So with tigers, he didn't get along
Jungle life was hard to get by
So he came to his friends at Ty.

Strut the Rooster

4th Generation

ty BEANIE ORIGINAL BABY

The Beanie Babies™ Collection
© Ty Inc.
Oakbrook IL, U.S.A.
© Ty UK Ltd.
Fareham, Hants
P015 5TX
© Ty Deutschland
90008 Nürnberg
Handmade in China

[Beanie Name]™ [Style Number]
DATE OF BIRTH: [Month-Day-Year]

[Beanie Poem]

Visit our web page!!!
http://www.ty.com

5th Generation

The Beanie Babies Collection
© Ty Inc.
Oakbrook, IL U.S.A
© Ty Europe Ltd
Fareham, Hants
P015 5TX
© Ty Canada
Aurora, Ontario
Handmade in China

ty BEANIE BABY

Please remove all swing tags
before giving this item to a child
Retain Tag For Reference
For ages 3 and up
Surface
Wash

[Beanie Name]™
DATE OF BIRTH: [Month-Day-Year]

[Beanie Poem]

www.ty.com

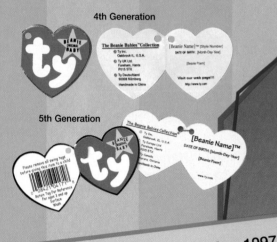

Strut made his debut in May 1997 as Doodle. His name was changed several months later to appease an unhappy fast-food franchise with a similar mascot named "Doodles."

Item #: 4171
Issued: 1997
Birthday: 3/8/96

Listen closely to "Cock-a-doodle-doo"
What's the rooster saying to you?
Hurry, wake up sleepy head
We have lots to do, get out of bed!

Tabasco the Bull

3rd Generation

ty

The Beanie Babies ™ Collection
© Ty Inc.
  Oakbrook IL. U.S.A.
© Ty UK Ltd.
  Waterlooville, Hants
  PO8 8HH
© Ty Deutschland
  90008 Nürnberg
  Handmade in China

[Beanie Name]™ [Style Number]
to _____
from _____
with
love

4th Generation

ty
BEANIE
ORIGINAL
BABY

The Beanie Babies™ Collection
© Ty Inc.
  Oakbrook IL. U.S.A.
© Ty UK Ltd.
  Fareham, Hants
  PO15 5TX
© Ty Deutschland
  90008 Nürnberg
  Handmade in China

[Beanie Name]™ [Style Number]
DATE OF BIRTH: [Month-Day-Year]

[Beanie Poem]

Visit our web page!!!
http://www.ty.com

Tabasco Hot Sauce Company may have had a problem with Tabasco's name and his red color. Ty retired Tabasco in January 1997 and reintroduced him in the form of Snort the Bull.

Item #: 4002
Issued: 1995
Retired: 1/97
Birthday: 5/15/95

Although Tabasco is not so tall
He loves to play basketball
He is a star player in his dream
Can you guess his favorite team?

Tank the Armadillo

3rd Generation

4th Generation

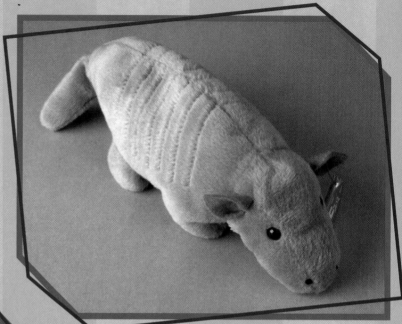

Tank the Armadillo was retired in October 1997. When Tank was introduced, he had nostrils and seven lines stitched on his back. Later he was changed to nine lines and nostrils with no shell. Finally stitches were added to the "rim" to emphasize a shell, and the nostrils were taken away.

Item #: 4031
Issued: 1995
Retired: 10/97
Birthday: 2/22/95

This armadillo lives in the South
Shoving Tex-Mex in his mouth
He sure loves it south of the border
Keeping his friends in good order!

1997 Teddy

4th Generation

The Beanie Babies™ Collection

© Ty Inc.
Oakbrook IL. U.S.A.

© Ty UK Ltd.
Fareham, Hants
PO15 5TX

© Ty Deutschland
90008 Nürnberg
Handmade in China

[Beanie Name]™ [Style Number]
DATE OF BIRTH: [Month-Day-Year]

[Beanie Poem]

Visit our web page!!!
http://www.ty.com

The "Holiday Bear" spent such a short time in stores — from October 1997 to January 1998 — that he's sure to be a valuable addition to any collection.

Item #: 4200
Issued: 1997
Retired: 1/98
Birthday: 12/25/96

Beanie Babies are special no doubt
All filled with love - inside and out
Wishes for fun times filled with joy
Ty's holiday teddy is a magical toy!

Teddy the Brown Teddy Bear
(Old - Old Face [left] , New - New Face [right])

1st Generation

The Beanie Babies Collection
[Beanie Name]™ [Style Number]
©1993 Ty Inc. Oakbrook, IL. USA
All Rights Reserved. Caution:
Remove this tag before giving
toy to a child. For ages 5 and up.
Handmade in Korea.
Surface
Wash

3rd Generation

The Beanie Babies.™ Collection
© Ty Inc.
Oakbrook IL. U.S.A.
© Ty UK Ltd.
Waterlooville, Hants
P08 8HH
© Ty Deutschland
90008 Nürnberg
Handmade in China

[Beanie Name]™ [Style Number
to _____
from ____
with
love

2nd Generation

The Beanie Babies Collection
© 1993 Ty Inc. Oakbrook, IL. U.S.A.
All Rights Reserved. Caution:
Remove this tag before giving
toy to a child. For ages 3 and up.
Handmade in China
Surface
Wash.

[Beanie Name]™ [Style Number]
to____
from____
with
love

4th Generation

The Beanie Babies™Collection
© Ty Inc.
Oakbrook IL. U.S.A.
© Ty UK Ltd.
Fareham, Hants
P015 5TX
© Ty Deutschland
90008 Nürnberg
Handmade in China

[Beanie Name]™ [Style Number]
DATE OF BIRTH : [Month-Day-Year]

[Beanie Poem]

Visit our web page!!!
http://www.ty.com

Brown Teddy joined his colored friends in retirement in October 1997. When the brown and colored Teddies were introduced, they had the classic Victorian teddy bear face (similar to the old Winnie the Pooh), which was later changed to the New Face of the pronounced snout.

Item #: 4050
Issued: 1994
Retired: 10/97
Birthday: 11/28/95

Teddy wanted to go out today
But all his friends went out to play
But he'd rather help whatever you do
After all, his best friend is you!

Teddy the Cranberry Teddy Bear

(Old - Old Face [left] , New - New Face [right])

1st Generation

The Beanie Babies Collection

[Beanie Name]™ [Style Number]
© 1993 Ty Inc. Oakbrook, IL. USA
All Rights Reserved. Caution:
Remove this tag before giving
toy to a child. For ages 5 and up.
Handmade in Korea.
Surface
Wash

2nd Generation

The Beanie Babies Collection

© 1993 Ty Inc. Oakbrook, IL. USA
All Rights Reserved. Caution:
Remove this tag before giving
toy to a child. For ages 3 and up.
Handmade in China
Surface
Wash

[Beanie Name]™ [Style Number]

to _____

from _____

with
love

3rd Generation

The Beanie Babies ™ Collection

© Ty Inc.
Oakbrook IL. U.S.A.

© Ty UK Ltd.
Waterlooville, Hants
PO8 8HH

© Ty Deutschland
90008 Nürnberg
Handmade in China

[Beanie Name]™ [Style Number]

to _____

from _____

with
love

The Teddies were first introduced with what is known as the "Old Face," which came to a point. The "New Face" is a pronounced snout with a bigger nose. Shortly after this reconstruction, the colored bears were retired in spring 1996, making the "New Face" bears more rare.

Poem: None

Item #: 4052

Issued: 1994

Retired: 1996

Birthday: Unknown

Teddy

the Jade Teddy Bear
(Old - Old Face [left] , New - New Face [right])

1st Generation

The Beanie Babies Collection

[Beanie Name]™ [Style Number]
© 1993 Ty Inc. Oakbrook, IL USA
All Rights Reserved. Caution:
Remove this tag before giving
toy to a child. For ages 5 and up.
Handmade in Korea.
Surface
Wash.

2nd Generation

The Beanie Babies Collection

© 1993 Ty Inc. Oakbrook, IL. USA
All Rights Reserved. Caution:
Remove this tag before giving
toy to a child. For ages 3 and up.
Handmade in China
Surface
Wash

[Beanie Name]™ [Style Number]
to _____
from _____
with
love

3rd Generation

The Beanie Babies™ Collection

® Ty Inc.
Oakbrook IL. U.S.A.
® Ty UK Ltd.
Waterlooville, Hants
PO8 8NH
® Ty Deutschland
90008 Nürnberg
Handmade in China

[Beanie Name]™ [Style Number]
to _____
from _____
with
love

Retired in spring 1996, the Jade bear appears more of a "hunter green."

Poem: None

Item #: 4057

Issued: 1994

Retired: 1996

Birthday: Unknown

Teddy

the Magenta Teddy Bear

(Old - Old Face [left] , New - New Face [right])

Retired in spring 1996, the Magenta bear looks more pink than its Cranberry counterpart, which appears more of a brick red.

1st Generation

ty

The Beanie Babies Collection
[Beanie Name]™ [Style Number]
©1993 Ty Inc. Oakbrook, IL. USA
All Rights Reserved. Caution
Remove this tag before giving
toy to a child. For ages 5 and up.
Handmade in Korea.
Surface
Wash.

2nd Generation

ty

The Beanie Babies Collection
© 1993 Ty Inc. Oakbrook, IL. USA
All Rights Reserved. Caution
Remove this tag before giving
toy to a child. For ages 3 and up.
Handmade in China
Surface
Wash.

[Beanie Name]™ [Style Number]
to _____
from _____
with
love

3rd Generation

ty **ty**

The Beanie Babies ™ Collection
Ⓣ Ty Inc.
Oakbrook IL. U.S.A.
Ⓣ Ty UK Ltd.
Waterlooville, Hants
POB 8HH
Ⓣ Ty Deutschland
90006 Nürnberg
Handmade in China

[Beanie Name]™ [Style Number]
to _____
from _____
with
love

Poem: None

Item #: 4056

Issued: 1994

Retired: 1996

Birthday: Unknown

Teddy the Teal Teddy Bear
(Old - Old Face [left] , New - New Face [right])

Retired in spring 1996, the Teal Teddy is more bright green than the Jade.

Poem: None

Item #: 4051

Issued: 1994

Retired: 1996

Birthday: Unknown

Teddy

the Violet Teddy Bear
(Old - Old Face [left] , New - New Face [right])

Violet Teddy retired
in spring 1996.

1st Generation

ty

The Beanie Babies Collection
[Beanie Name]™ [Style Number]
© 1993 Ty Inc. Oakbrook, IL. USA
All Rights Reserved. Caution:
Remove this tag before giving
toy to a child. For ages 5 and up.
Handmade in Korea.
Surface
Wash

2nd Generation

ty

The Beanie Babies Collection
© 1993 Ty Inc. Oakbrook, IL. USA
All Rights Reserved. Caution:
Remove this tag before giving
toy to a child. For ages 3 and up.
Handmade in China
Surface
Wash.

[Beanie Name]™ [Style Number]
to ____
from ____
with
love

3rd Generation

ty

The Beanie Babies ™ Collection
© Ty Inc.
Oakbrook IL. U.S.A.
Ty UK Ltd.
Waterlooville, Hants
P08 8HH
Ty Deutschland
90008 Nürnberg
Handmade in China

[Beanie Name]™ [Style Number]
to ____
from ____
with
love

Poem: None

Item #: 4055
Issued: 1994
Retired: 1996
Birthday: Unknown

125

Trap the Mouse

1st Generation

The Beanie Babies Collection
[Beanie Name]™ [Style Number]
© 1993 Ty Inc. Oakbrook, IL, USA
All Rights Reserved. Caution:
Remove this tag before giving
toy to a child. For ages 5 and up.
Handmade in Korea.
Surface
Wash.

2nd Generation

The Beanie Babies Collection
© 1993 Ty Inc. Oakbrook, IL, USA
All Rights Reserved. Caution:
Remove this tag before giving
toy to a child. For ages 3 and up.
Handmade in China
Surface
Wash.

[Beanie Name]™ [Style Number]
to _____
from _____
with
love

3rd Generation

The Beanie Babies™ Collection
© Ty Inc.
Oakbrook IL. U.S.A
© Ty UK Ltd.
Waterlooville, Hants
P08 9HII
© Ty Deutschland
90008 Nürnberg
Handmade in China

[Beanie Name]™ [Style Number]
to _____
from _____
with
love

Trap the Mouse retired in spring 1996.

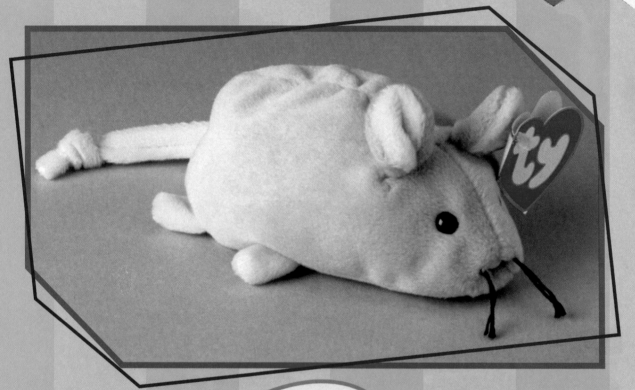

Poem: None

Item #: 4042
Issued: 1994
Retired: 1996
Birthday: Unknown

Tuffy the Brown Terrier

4th Generation

5th Generation

Tuffy is one of the few napped Beanies in the collection.

Item #: 4108
Issued: 1997
Birthday: 10/12/96

Taking off with a thunderous blast
Tuffy rides his motorcycle fast
The Beanies roll with laughs and squeals
He never took off his training wheels!

Tusk the Walrus

3rd Generation

The Beanie Babies™ Collection
ⓐ Ty Inc.
Oakbrook IL. U.S.A.
ⓐ Ty UK Ltd.
Waterlooville, Hants
P08 8HH
ⓐ Ty Deutschland
90008 Nürnberg
Handmade in China

[Beanie Name]™ [Style Numb
to
from
with
love

4th Generation

The Beanie Babies™ Collection
ⓐ Ty Inc.
Oakbrook IL. U.S.A.
ⓐ Ty UK Ltd.
Fareham, Hants
P015 5TX
ⓐ Ty Deutschland
90008 Nürnberg
Handmade in China

[Beanie Name]™ [Style Number]
DATE OF BIRTH: [Month-Day-Year]

[Beanie Poem]

Visit our web page!!!
http://www.ty.com

Tusk the Walrus was retired in January 1997 to make way for Jolly the Walrus. Jolly is much more detailed than Tusk.

Item #: 4076
Issued: 1995
Birthday: Unknown
Retired: 1/97

Tusk brushes his teeth everyday
To keep them shiny, it's the only way
Teeth are special, so you must try
And they will sparkle when you say "Hi"!

Twigs the Giraffe

A Twigs with a third-generation tag is significantly more expensive than a current one.

3rd Generation

The Beanie Babies ™ Collection
© Ty Inc.
Oakbrook IL. U.S.A.
© Ty UK Ltd.
Waterlooville, Hants
PO8 8HH
© Ty Deutschland
90008 Nürnberg
Handmade in China

[Beanie Name]™ [Style Number]
to _____
from _____
with
love

4th Generation

The Beanie Babies™ Collection
© Ty Inc.
Oakbrook IL. U.S.A.
© Ty UK Ltd.
Farnham, Hants
PO15 5TX
© Ty Deutschland
90008 Nürnberg
Handmade in China

[Beanie Name]™ [Style Number]
DATE OF BIRTH: [Month-Day-Year]

[Beanie Poem]

Visit our web pages!!!
http://www.ty.com

5th Generation

The Beanie Babies Collection
© Ty Inc.
Oakbrook, IL. U.S.A.
© Ty Europe Ltd
Fareham, Hants
PO15 5TX
© Ty Canada
Aurora, Ontario
Handmade in China

[Beanie Name]™
DATE OF BIRTH: [Month-Day-Year]

[Beanie Poem]

www.Ty.com

Please remove all swing tags
before giving this item to a child

Batten Tag For Reference
For ages 3 and up
Surface
Wash

Item #: 4068
Issued: 1995
Birthday: 5/19/95

Twigs has his head in the clouds
He stands tall, he stands proud
With legs so skinny they wobble and shake
What an unusual friend he will make!

Valentino the Bear

2nd Generation

The Beanie Babies Collection

© 1993 Ty Inc. Oakbrook, IL. USA
All Rights Reserved. Caution
Remove this tag before giving
toy to a child. For ages 3 and up.
Handmade in China
Surface
Wash.

[Beanie Name]™ [Style Number]

to _____

from _____

with
love

3rd Generation

The Beanie Babies ™ Collection

© Ty Inc.
Oakbrook IL. U.S.A.

© Ty UK Ltd.
Waterlooville, Hants
P08 8HH

© Ty Deutschland
90008 Nürnberg
Handmade in China

[Beanie Name]™ [Style Number]

to _____

from _____
with
love

4th Generation

The Beanie Babies™Collection

© Ty Inc.
Oakbrook IL. U.S.A.

© Ty UK Ltd.
Fareham, Hants
P015 5TX

© Ty Deutschland
90008 Nürnberg
Handmade in China

[Beanie Name]™ [Style Number]

DATE OF BIRTH: [Month-Day-Year]

[Beanie Poem]

Visit our web page!!!
http://www.ty.com

5th Generation

Please remove all swing tags
before giving this item to a child

Before Tag For Reference
For ages 3 and up
Surface
Wash

The Beanie Babies Collection
© Ty Inc.
Oakbrook, IL. U.S.A.
© Ty Europe Ltd.
Fareham, Hants
P015 5TX
Ty Canada
Aurora, Ontario
Handmade in China

[Beanie Name]™
DATE OF BIRTH: [Month-Day-Year]

[Beanie Poem]

www.ty.com

Although a favorite gift for Valentine's Day, Valentino is rumored as a likely retirement.

Item #: 4058

Issued: 1994

Birthday: 2/14/94

His heart is red and full of love
He cares for you so give him a hug
Keep him close when feeling blue
Feel the love he has for you!

Velvet the Panther

3rd Generation

The Beanie Babies™ Collection

© Ty Inc.
Oakbrook IL U.S.A.

© Ty UK Ltd.
Waterlooville, Hants
PO8 8NH

© Ty Deutschland
90008 Nürnberg

Handmade in China

[Beanie Name]™ [Style Number]

to _____
from _____
with
love

4th Generation

The Beanie Babies™ Collection

© Ty Inc.
Oakbrook IL U.S.A.

© Ty UK Ltd.
Fareham, Hants
PO15 5TX

© Ty Deutschland
90008 Nürnberg

Handmade in China

[Beanie Name]™ [Style Number]
DATE OF BIRTH : [Month-Day-Year]

[Beanie Poem]

Visit our web page!!!
http://www.ty.com

Velvet the Panther was retired in October 1997.

Item #:   4064
Issued: 1995
Retired: 10/97
Birthday: 12/16/95

Velvet loves to sleep in the trees
Lulled to dreams by the buzz of the bees
She snoozes all day and plays all night
Running and jumping in the moonlight!

Waddle the Penguin

3rd Generation

4th Generation

5th Generation

Everyone loves penguins, and Waddle is no exception.

Item #: 4075
Issued: 1995
Birthday: 12/19/95

Waddle the penguin likes to dress up
Every night he wears his tux
When Waddle walks, it never fails
He always trips over his tails!

Waves
the Orca Whale

4th Generation

5th Generation

In May 1997, Waves became the replacement for the newly retired Splash the Whale. Waves has a curved body, whereas Splash lays flat.

Item #: 4084
Issued: 1997
Birthday: 12/8/96

Join him today on the Internet
Don't be afraid to get your feet wet
He taught all the Beanies how to surf
Our web page is his home turf!

Web the Spider

1st Generation

The Beanie Babies Collection
[Beanie Name]™ [Style Number]
©1993 Ty Inc. Oakbrook, IL USA
All Rights Reserved. Caution:
Remove this tag before giving
toy to a child. For ages 5 and up.
Handmade in Korea.
Surface
Wash

2nd Generation

The Beanie Babies Collection
© 1993 Ty Inc. Oakbrook, IL. USA
All Rights Reserved. Caution:
Remove this tag before giving
toy to a child. For ages 3 and up.
Handmade in China
Surface
Wash.
[Beanie Name]™ [Style Number]
to _____
from _____
with
love

3rd Generation

The Beanie Babies™ Collection
® Ty Inc.
Oakbrook IL. U.S.A.
® Ty UK Ltd.
Waterlooville, Hants
P06 8HH
® Ty Deutschland
90008 Nürnberg
Handmade in China
[Beanie Name]™ [Style Number]
to _____
from _____
with
love

Web the Spider retired
in the fall of 1996.

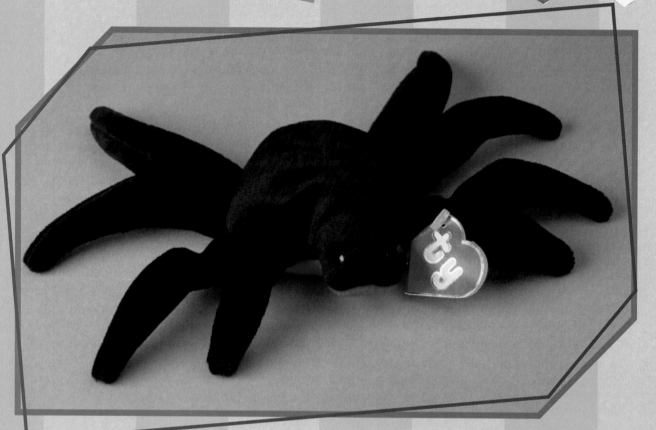

Poem: None

Item #: 4041
Issued: 1994
Retired: 1996
Birthday: Unknown

Weenie the Dachshund

Terminally cute, Weenie remains popular despite his easy-to-find status.

Item #: 4013
Issued: 1996
Birthday: 7/20/95

Weenie the dog is quite a sight
Long of body and short of height
He perches himself high on a log
And considers himself to be top dog!

Wrinkles the Bulldog

Wrinkles' wrinkly hide makes him a favorite of Beanie dog collectors.

Item #: 4103
Issued: 1996
Birthday: 5/1/96

This little dog is named Wrinkles
His nose is soft and often crinkles
Likes to climb up on your lap
He's a cheery sort of chap!

Ziggy the Zebra

Kids, especially, love the black-and-white striped Ziggy.

Item #: 4063
Issued: 1995
Birthday: 12/24/95

Ziggy likes soccer - he's a referee
That way he watches the games for free
The other Beanies don't think it's fair
But Ziggy the zebra doesn't care.

Zip the Black Cat (Old - Black with White Face & Belly [top left], Old - All Black [top right], New - Black with White Paws)

Zip, like Nip, has had three lives. Zip has been all black, black with a white face and belly, and black with white paws.

2nd Generation

3rd Generation

4th Generation

5th Generation

Item #: 4004
Issued: 1994
Birthday: 3/28/94

Keep Zip by your side all the day through
Zip is good luck, you'll see it's true
When you have something you need to do
Zip will always believe in you!

Generations

Old tag or new? The difference can mean hundreds of dollars.

by Vicky Krupka

A s every collector knows, or should know, Ty Beanie Babies are produced with both a heart-shaped "swing" tag and a sewn-in "tush" tag. The condition and generation of the tags greatly affect a Beanie's value. For proof, take a quick glance at the price guide on page 48. Animals that are identical in every detail except their tags vary widely in their values.

Clearly, one of the first and most crucial things for a collector to learn is the difference between the generations of swing and tush tags. To date, there are four generations of each.

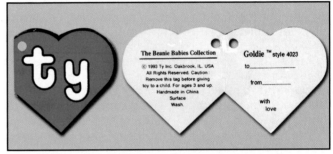

Swing (Heart) Tag - Second generation

Swing (Heart) Tag - First generation

Swing (Heart) Tags

In 1994 when the first nine Beanie Babies were introduced (Legs, Bones, Flash, Splash, Patti, Chocolate, Squealer, Cubbie and Pinchers), they wore what is referred to as "first generation" tags. The first generation swing tag is a "single heart" that was produced in 1994 only. The front is red with the letters "ty" in white, trimmed in gold. On the back of the tag appears the Beanie's style number, name and information about where it was produced.

The second generation swing tag was introduced later in 1994. It is the same size as the first generation with the same skinny "ty" letters on it, except that it is a "double heart," which opens up. On the inside left is copyright information, and on the right is the Beanie's name, style number and, if distributed in the United States, the words to_____ and from_____.

Ty introduced the third generation swing tag in mid-1995 at the same time as the second generation tush tag. This third generation swing tag is slightly larger than the first two. Although the heart and the letters "ty" are still edged in gold, the lettering is much larger. The inside of the tag remained much the same with copyright information on the left side and the

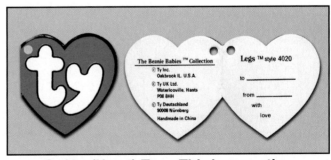

Swing (Heart) Tag - Third generation

Beanie's name, style number, to_____ and from_____ on the right side.

The fourth generation swing tag was introduced in mid-1996 at the same time as the third generation tush tag. The "ty" letters are still the larger size, but no longer edged in gold. Included on the front is a yellow star with the words "Original Beanie Baby" inside it. Inside the tag, the left side remained the same, but the right side now included a date of birth and a

139

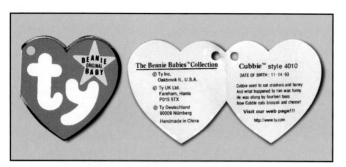

Swing (Heart) Tag - Fourth generation

specialized poem for the Beanie, as well as its name and style number.

It was with the introduction of these tags that Ty started including its website information. (Note: The date on the tush tag does not relate to the "birthday" assigned by Ty to the Beanies. Instead, it relates to the year that a particular Beanie or style of Beanie was first designed.)

The fifth generation swing tag appeared in 1998. The outside of the tag remains much the same except for a change in the typeface used for the words "Original Beanie Baby" located inside the yellow star and the wording on the back.

Inside the tag, the font has changed to the same font as the outside of the tag. On the left side the phrase "The Beanie Babies Collection" has a trademark (TM) symbol after the entire phrase, and no registered mark (®) after

the word Babies. The rest of the address information for Ty Inc., Ty Europe and Ty Canada remain the same. (Note Ty UK and Ty Deutschland were combined into Ty Europe late in 1997, thus leaving room on the tag to add the Ty Canada information.)

The most noticeable changes have taken place on the right-hand side of the tag. The Beanie's style number is no longer given (although it still appears in the UPC code

Swing (Heart) Tag - Fifth generation

on the back), and the Beanie's name is centered at the top. Double-spaced below the Beanie's name is the date of birth, but the month and year are now fully spelled out rather than given in numeric shorthand. Additionally the bottom of the tag, which previously said "Visit our web page!!! http://www.ty.com," now reads simply "www.ty.com".

Beanie Babies Condition Guide

Before you buy or sell, learn to judge a Beanie's condition

by Kim Goddard

The expanding secondary market for Beanie Babies means collectors who aren't armed with a solid understanding of its terms are at a distinct disadvantage.

With Tags. Without Tags. Mint. Slightly Used. You might run into a "bent tag" Patti or a "slightly bent tag" Peanut. Some sellers bill their Beanies as coming from "a smoke-free-environment." Do these conditions affect the quality of the Beanie about to be purchased? Certainly! Here is a quick run-through of how to be a connoisseur of the Beanie Baby secondary market.

Three major factors determine the value of a Beanie Baby: the tags, the condition of the plush, and the condition of the Beanie itself.

The Swing Tag is one of the first determining factors of value. Everyone would like a mint Beanie Baby,

but in the secondary market that may not always be possible. Especially with rare Beanie Babies, the chances are good that the swing tag is missing or damaged This happened quite often before people became aware of the collectibility of Beanies. The animal probably started life as a child's plaything, so the parents naturally cut off the tags.

A current Beanie without its swing tag is worth about half the retail price or less. A recently retired Beanie that runs around the hundred-dollar range in mint condition usually receives a fifty percent markdown without the tag.

The fifty percent rule does not apply with the older retirees. Some purchasers, who may have searched months for a particular Beanie, may not care if there's a swing tag or not. There is a decrease in price, but

First Generation Tush Tag

Tush (Sewn-In) Tags

The first generation tush tag is white with black printing. On the tag is copyright and materials information. This tag was in use from 1994 to mid-1996.

The second generation tush tag is white with red

Second Generation Tush Tag

printing and was introduced mid-year 1995. On one side of it is the Ty heart logo, and on the other is copyright and materials information.

The third generation tush tag was introduced mid-1996. It is white with red printing, but this time the Ty heart logo is smaller, and the name of the Beanie is also

Third Generation Tush Tag

printed on the tag. On the back is copyright and materials information.

The fourth generation tush tag was introduced mid-year 1997. It is identical to the third generation tush tag, except that there now appears a small red star at the upper left corner of the Ty heart.

An additional tush tag that appears on Beanies, and

not so steep. A good example of this is the Spot without the spot. In mint condition, this particular Spot is worth around $1,000. Without the swing tag, Spot without the spot can bring in around $700.

Sometimes the tush tag may be missing as well. In this case, the value is cut drastically (usually by sixty percent and higher), since there is no actual proof that this Beanie is a real Ty Beanie Baby.

If the swing tag is damaged (meaning creased, worn, frayed edges, torn) the markdown depends on the severity. Mild damage (slightly creased) would cause a drop of $10 to $50, depending on the status or rarity of the Beanie. An obviously damaged tag would decrease the value by as much as a fourth of the mint price. Most of the time, a severely damaged tag (creased or torn) is considered barely a step above a missing tag.

Keep in mind that many parents remove the tag from a Beanie for safekeeping. The tag may be replaced later to sell the Beanie. It's hard to determine just how much to knock off the value of a Beanie such as this. Technically, it's no longer mint. This is where the condition of the plush should be considered. If the tag looks fine but the plush is worn, the Beanie probably has been retagged, and the price should decrease by about a fourth.

Collectors also may wonder how to treat a Beanie with a price sticker on the tag. For the most part, this is a little annoyance that must be tolerated and doesn't affect the value, although a sticker in plain view on the front of the tag can depreciate it a little. Attempting to remove the sticker can result in tearing the tag, however, so it's best to leave it alone.

Another factor in determining the value of a Beanie Baby is the quality of its plush. Look for traces of dirt, fibers that aren't shiny (or even a little clumped), and any signs of stitching or repair. If the fibers are clumped and smell like Tide, the Beanie has been washed.

In the case of worn plush, the only real guide is your own best judgment. A good starting point, if it is obviously worn, is half the mint value.

One factor often overlooked is a Beanie Baby's environment. Though they don't look like sponges, that is exactly what Beanie Babies are. They absorb smells, smoke and other airborne particles. If the Beanie has an odor or its plush has become discolored, it is no longer mint. The value should be decreased by about a third, for starters.

A Beanie Baby's value is determined by its tags, its plush and its environment. Every situation will be different, and the guidelines for marking down the value may not always hold. Examine the Beanie, make sure that the felt is smooth and feels clean (and not sticky), and smell it for unusual odors. Rub your fingers across the tags to find creases you may not see. Then decide what you feel the Beanie is worth and make an offer.

Fourth Generation Tush Tag

often confuses collectors, is the Canadian tag. This is attached to the Beanie in addition to the Ty tush tag. It is slightly larger and printed in black ink. The tag is required by Canadian law for stuffed articles sold in Canada and is printed in both French and English. This larger tag was even attached to Canadian Teenie Beanies.

Fifth Generation Tush Tag

To date, Ty has made some kind of change to the swing and/or tush tag each year, usually in the middle of the year when new Beanies are released. A slight exception occurred when the May 11, 1997, new releases (Jolly, Waves, Echo, Tuffy, Pugsly, Chip, Claude, Roary, Peace, Nanook, Blizzard, Baldy and Doodle), appeared without any change to the tush tag. To amend this, Ty attached a clear sticker with a small red star over existing tush tags. This converted them into temporary fourth generation tags.

What's in a Name?

Amazing as it seems, a small change in the name on a Beanie's swing or tush tag can greatly affect its value.

Due to the mass production of Beanie Babies, it is extremely common to find Beanies with wrong swing and/or tush tags. That is, the name on the tag(s) does not match the actual name of the Beanie. To the chagrin of many collectors who purchase these mistags thinking they have found a rare item, the mistake generally reduces the value of the Beanie. Most collectors consider mistags less desirable, especially once the Beanie becomes retired. A wrong swing tag, because of the ease with which they are switched, can reduce the value of a Beanie Baby by 40 to 50 percent. A wrong tush tag can reduce a Beanie's value as much as 30 or 40 percent.

As with most rules, there are always exceptions.

Some of the more notable tag mistakes that have actuall increased the Beanie's value are: Snort, who appeared wit Tabasco swing tags when first released; Sparky, wh appeared with Dotty tush tags before Dotty was intro duced; and Echo and Waves, who debuted in the Unite States wearing each other's swing and tush tags!

In a few instances, Beanies have undergone nam changes just prior to release or soon after release, suc as Nana, Brownie, Pride and Doodle, none of which appea on Ty Inc.'s "official" list of Beanie Babies.

Nana is the name first given to Bongo. It was change after production but prior to release. Since the swin tags were already printed with the name "Nana," T covered it up with a sticker that had Bongo's name printe on it.

Brownie is Cubbie's original name. Brownie appear on very few Beanies, thus making it highly a sough variation. In both instances, the swing tag carries abou

Canadian Tush Tag

95% of the value of the Beanie. Without swing tags, ther is no way of knowing whether the Beanie was original ly named Nana instead of Bongo, or if it was a rare Browni versus a common Cubbie. Thus, a $900 Nana or Browni without a swing tag is worth no more than an ordinar Bongo or Cubbie.

Pride is the name that was originally given to th Canadian bear, Maple. Prior to Pride's release, the nam became Maple, but not before about 3,000 of the bear had been produced with Pride tush tags. Referred to a Maple/Pride, these "mistake" Beanies are worth as muc as four times more than Maple with both tags correct

Doodle is the fourth Beanie to undergo a name chang after being released to the public, but the swap did no occur until a large number had been produced. Becaus of the similarity to a fast food chain's mascot name "Doodles," Ty changed the name of their rooster to Stru The new name instantly made Doodle more valuable an sought after, despite being identical to Strut, its re placement.

The misspelling of a Beanie's name on the swing ta can also increase a Beanie's value, as the mistake is usuall caught early in the production run. The three most wel known spelling mistakes that are considered more valuab are "Tuck" (instead of Tusk) the Walrus; Spook (instea of Spooky) the Ghost; and "Punchers" (instead of Pincher the Lobster.

The fifth generation tush tag remains the same a those that first appeared on the October 1997 new release At that time, Ty introduced changes to the 4th versio tush tags relating to the trademark symbols. "Beani Babies" has the trademark registration ® after it, an the entire phrase "The Beanie Babies Collection" is followe by the TM symbol. There is also an additional trademar symbol after the Beanie's name on the tush tag.

The Care & Feeding of Beanie Babies

A few simple guidelines to keep your collection in top shape

by Vicky Krupka

A large part of the appeal of Beanie Babies is their dual nature: both a toy and a collectible. Remove one part of the equation, and their immense popularity fades to nothing.

If, for example, Ty operated as most toy makers, Beanies would have been tossed onto the pop culture trash heap long ago. Production would have ramped up as quickly as demand, and values on the secondary market would have plummeted to retail or less, rendering Beanie Babies just another Cabbage Patch or Tickle Me Elmo blink-and-you'll-miss-it fad.

On the other hand, Beanie Babies' status as toys is one of the keys to their success. The market is choked with collectibles that serve no purpose other than to fill collectors' display cases and manufacturers' coffers. While there is nothing intrinsically wrong with these products, they just lack that certain "something" – call it personality – that has allowed Beanie Babies to rise above the pack.

Unfortunately, the toy/collectible nature of Beanie Babies also carries an inherent conflict.

Simply displaying a collection means you miss a chance to truly enjoy it, while playing with Beanies puts them at risk of becoming soiled or damaged and, thus, less collectible. While we can't answer this "display or play" question for you, we can offer a few suggestions for whichever course you choose.

Most container stores sell acrylic cubes for display purposes.

Displaying A Collection

If your collection is for display only, it should be placed where the Beanies will receive the most protection. This means a location where they will not be exposed to the sun, odors or moisture. It also means protecting the tags from becoming bent or creased.

A favorite method of displaying Beanie Babies is in an enclosed curio cabinet. This will keep the Beanies out of harm's way while also protecting them from the elements. Another method of display that is becoming popular is the use of acrylic boxes that completely enclose the Beanie yet still allow it to be viewed. These acrylic boxes can be found in a variety of sizes in most container stores.

To give the swing tag additional protection, you might want to use a tag protector. There are several types currently available. The most common is a hard acrylic locket that encases the tag, although there also are soft poly "sleeves" that slip over the tag. Both completely cover the tag and provide protection from dirt, bending and creasing while the tag is attached to the Beanie.

Protecting A Tag

If the Beanie is going to be handled, you should consider removing the swing tag first. A Beanie's value is reduced by as much as 50 percent if it is missing the swing tag, and a creased and/or torn tag

Remove tags from Beanies destined for the toy box or the washer.

can reduce the value just as much.

A severely damaged tag is considered the equivalent of no tag at all. By removing the tag, you can keep it in mint condition, and it can be easily re-attached later.

Removal of the swing tag does not mean you have to cut the plastic

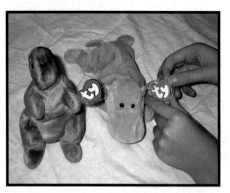

Tag protectors will keep a swing tag safe from creases.

connector. To remove the tag and preserve the connector for future re-attachment, simply slide the connector out through the hole in which it was inserted. This may take some practice, especially with fuzzier Beanies or ones where the tag is attached in a difficult place, such as in Pugsly's curled up ear or Seaweed's arm.

When you are unable (or simply reluctant) to remove the swing tag, use a protector to help keep the tag in good condition.

What should you do if the Beanie Baby you just bought or traded for is clean, but smells of cigarette smoke? Rather than put it through the stress of washing, try this trick to remove the smell: Place the Beanie into a closed container or Ziplock baggie along with some newspaper or an open box of baking soda. Seal the container shut and let it sit for a couple of days. With luck, the newspaper or baking soda will absorb the smell.

Removing Stickers

Most Beanie Babies disappear from store shelves too fast for retailers to bother putting price stickers on them. However, some stores do take the time to place stickers on swing tags, which collectors then feel compelled to remove.

Because a price sticker is part of the "history" of the Beanie, and removal of it can cause damage to the swing tag, we recommend leaving the sticker on the tag. A price sticker on the back side of a swing tag will not affect the value of the Beanie Baby. Nevertheless, when selling or trading a Beanie with a price sticker the sticker's existence should be mentioned to the buyer. A more serious problem is a partially removed sticker, which can leave an unsightly sticky residue on the tag. It is possible to remove this residue if great care is taken.

First, soften the glue by using a blow dryer. Put the dryer on medium heat and aim at the sticker until it is soft enough to peel off. To remove any remaining glue, use either lighter fluid, or a solvent such as Goo Gone. Warning! These products can also remove the ink and color from the tag, so use them sparingly. It is best to put a small amount of the fluid on a Q-tip and lightly rub only the affected area. With care, most of the stickiness can be removed and you will have a tag with a nice appearance again.

So, whether your collection is safely tucked away or scattered on the floor, following these few simple rules and precautions should keep it looking nice for years to come.

Dealing With Dirt

Over time, it is natural for "loved" Beanie Babies to become dirty. You should not have to live with a dirty Beanie out of fear that washing it will ruin it. With certain precautions, it is safe to wash a Beanie Baby either by hand or in the washing machine.

The first precaution, of course, is to remove the swing tag. The second is almost as obvious: Don't immerse Beanies with felt or glued-on features in water. These should be surface or "spot" washed. Just two Beanies have glued-on parts -- the seven-dot Lucky and Spooky with the red felt mouth. Felt, since it is not a woven fabric, is easily stretched out of shape when wet, which is why it should not be washed. Some Beanies that have felt features are: Radar (hands and legs), Crunch (teeth), Seaweed (piece of "seaweed"), Doodle/Strut (wattles), Lizzy (tongue), Bucky (teeth), Lucky (feet), Grunt (spines) and Tank (ears).

To hand wash a Beanie, soak it in warm water with a mild detergent. If the Beanie is extremely dirty, let it soak a little longer and "swish" it around in the water to loosen up particles of dirt. Afterward, thoroughly rinse the Beanie in warm water, and then either let it air dry or blow it dry with a hair dryer.

Machine washed Beanies should be tied inside a pillowcase to protect their eyes and noses from scratches. Use the gentle cycle. Again, the Beanie can be either air dried, blow dried, or placed in the dryer. If using the dryer, keep the Beanie inside the pillow case and dry at a low temperature. Once the Beanie is dry, restore some of the original "fluffiness" by lightly brushing it with a fabric lint brush or a toothbrush. (Hint: if the Beanie being washed has whiskers, you can apply a very tiny amount of watered down, clear craft glue to the tips of the whiskers to prevent fraying.)

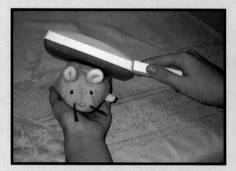

After a trip to the washer, a Beanie should be dried and its nap restored with a lint brush or toothbrush.